Cool Cooking for Kids

RECIPES AND NUTRITION FOR PRESCHOOLERS

Pat McClenahan

DIRECTOR, HARMONY PLAYHOUSE
NURSERY SCHOOL AND KINDERGARTEN,
NORTH HOLLYWOOD, CALIFORNIA

Ida Jaqua, M.A.

HOME ECONOMICS DEPARTMENT,
LOS ANGELES VALLEY COLLEGE,
VAN NUYS, CALIFORNIA

David S. Lake Publishers

Belmont, California

This book is dedicated to Huldah Champion, former Assistant Professor of Home Economics at Los Angeles Valley College, who has been the inspiration for so many who are now working in the field of early-childhood development.

Edited by Judith Quinn
Designed and illustrated by Eleanor Mennick
Puppetry by Betsy Brown
Photography by Frank Berry

ISBN-0-8224-1614-X
Library of Congress Catalog Card Number: 75-32841
Printed in the United States of America

CONTENTS

PREFACE

This is not just a cookbook—rather, it is a guide for teaching cooking and nutrition creatively. It is our hope that the lesson plans, the recipes, and the enrichment activities offered here will enable teachers to teach cooking and nutrition as they do any subject matter in today's schools—that is, by defining objectives, developing lesson plans, and evaluating the outcomes of specific learning experiences.

The recipes in Chapter 3 and Chapter 4 appear within the context of lesson plans, with suggestions for varying the ingredients and the methods of preparation, as well as enrichment activities that relate particular foods and cooking experiences to other areas of preschool learning, such as art, science, nature, music, math, and social studies.

Our unique Chapter 3, "Real Cool Cooking," offers a rich collection of recipes and cooking activities that preschoolers can enjoy without using heat, and Chapter 4, "Cool Cooking with Heat," provides a further 70 pages of recipes and activities for children between two years old and kindergarten age—this time using heat. These recipes appear in a step-by-step format easy for teachers and children to follow. Preschool cooking and nutrition lessons can be great fun. We hope this format and the detailed explanations in the accompanying lesson plans will encourage teachers who are inexperienced in cooking to make some attempts at working with food in their classes. They may be surprised at how much young children can accomplish!

All recipes have been tested and found "childworthy." They have been chosen both because they are interesting to preschoolers and because they are easy to prepare in nursery and primary schools. The ages of the children each recipe suits are noted clearly. Children can perform all operations except those which are identified as being "for teachers" by the symbol ♆.

General methods for teaching cooking to preschoolers appear in Chapter 1, "Cooking Is Kid Stuff," along with the suggestions for activities that will prepare the children for this new experience. The chapter also offers patterns for the cooking puppets, Ms. Parsley and Mr. Hush Puppy, some of the teacher's best aids. Novices at cooking will find the review of measuring and equivalents helpful, and anyone who is setting up or expanding a cooking center for young children will benefit from the evaluation of equipment.

Nutrition and health, our second major emphasis, is an important area of learning that has been woefully neglected in schools—and especially in the early years. Preschoolers *can* learn about foods and their nutritional value, and that knowledge will be important to them throughout their lives. Chapter 2, "Nutrition and Health," which reviews the subject for teachers, also suggests teaching approaches that work with young children, as well as describing related games and activities preschoolers enjoy. In addition, many sources of information and teaching aids, in government and in private industry, are listed in the back of the book.

As in any book that represents a cooperative effort, appreciation and thanks are due to many people. First and foremost are the children of the many nursery schools who have tried our ideas, the students of Los Angeles Valley College in Van Nuys, California, who have given us their suggestions, and the teachers of Harmony Playhouse in North Hollywood, California, who have enthusiastically worked with the program. We also wish to express our appreciation to Bea Stern, Associate Professor of Child Development at Los Angeles Valley College for her helpful suggestions.

Cooking Is Kid Stuff

TEACHING COOKING TO PRESCHOOLERS

Pleasure in eating is one of the first recognizable carry-overs from home to nursery school. Nursery schools can exploit this in a positive way to make themselves seem more familiar to children, by including cooking and eating in their programs. We form our attitudes about food very early in life, and those attitudes can be influenced by the people around us. Nursery schools can help children develop good attitudes, and they can also expand children's knowledge of foods beyond what they have experienced at home.

In this day of convenience foods, many children have only limited knowledge of foods, where they come from, and how to prepare them. Hundreds of volumes have been written for adults on the rewards of combining raw food materials to achieve sublime, gourmet results, with the added joy of sharing those results. Yet, few children today have opportunities to shop for, prepare, and serve food. What a deprivation! Children enjoy the smells and the appearances of food. And they enjoy handling it. Like adults, they get pleasure from its textures, colors, and tastes.

They also enjoy the social contact of cooking and eating with parents, teachers, and other children. We all have pleasant memories associated with food—of family dinners, of holidays, of visits with friends and relatives, and of picnics, vacations, and other trips. The same kinds of feelings can be realized for children in simple, everyday experiences with food.

Adults too often regard the preparation of food as ordinary, without recognizing how exciting just the change from the raw state to the cooked state can be for children, or how wonderful it might seem to children to act out their parents' roles in this activity, which is so basic to life and to daily living.

It is not difficult to provide cooking experiences in nursery or primary schools, since lessons can be set up almost anywhere—inside or out—with a minimum of equipment. Foods can and should be cooked in school for the children to eat on the spot, to share with others, and to take home. Children should be encouraged to discuss such experiences with their parents, so their whole families can share their new interest. Teachers can reinforce this by suggesting that parents inquire about their children's cooking experiences at school, or by posting bulletin boards to show what the children have been doing each day so parents can see them when they collect the children. Home and school can reinforce each other, and cooking experiences should be frequent in both.

Nursery-school teachers often hear mothers saying it is impossible to prepare dinner with the children underfoot demanding attention. Our plan is to make it possible for mothers to succeed in their role of providing food for the families while, at the same time, spending time with their children, who are busy, happy, and creative. We do this by teaching cooking skills and knowledge of foods that enable children to work constructively in the kitchen. We believe it is logical for parents to allow the children to work in the kitchen right along with them, since they must prepare dinner and the children want to be with them at that time. It actually takes much less time and energy to teach children to work in the kitchen than to try to push them away or to ignore them. And, of course, it is far more rewarding.

There are ways of adjusting to the lack of time and energy at the end of the day, as well as to the inevitable mess. For example, mothers can plan special nights for cooking together for which the children can select the menus, they can plan simple meals the children can help with each evening, they can take the children shopping with them (using preplanned shopping lists), or they can plan specific tasks for the children to perform in preparing all or some of the family meals.

Even though woman's place in society is changing, she is still the main preparer of food. But a more important consideration is the happiness of her children. It is our contention that the two concerns can be combined and met successfully. For this reason, we feel experiences with cooking and nutrition in school can be especially important for the children of working mothers.

Guidelines for Teaching The first cooking experience for preschoolers should be simple and without hazard. For this it is best to limit cooking groups to between eight and twelve children per teacher. Both children and teachers should start with elementary procedures and work up to more complicated cooking experiences as progress takes place. It is also best to begin with foods the children know and like, and then branch out later. You will find many suggestions for safe and easy projects in Chapter 3, "Real Cool Cooking."

As the children progress, review what they have learned as often as seems necessary. By building on learning they have already mastered, the children can progress to the more complicated techniques. Remember that these cooking lessons may be some children's first cooperative endeavors, so you will probably have to repeat your detailed explanations and demonstrations fairly often.

In planning curriculum, be sure it is geared to what the children can accomplish. (Recipes here are identified by what ages they suit.) Expect two-year-olds to be uncoordinated and messy. Therefore, do not fill cups too full, do not get upset by their characteristic messiness, and keep a sponge handy for easy cleanup (in a place where the children can reach it). In the first lessons let the children know their assistance in cleaning up is part of the job—and fun, too, because it is a shared activity.

Remember that these cooking experiences are for the development of the children, so allow them to participate in as many of the activities as possible. In our recipes the few operations that children can't do are identified by the symbol ♀ for "teacher."

The children know very little about cooking, and whatever experiences do take place are new and very exciting to them, so make them fun! As in any experience with young children, the teacher's enthusiasm for the subject will be contagious. Whether success or failure is the result is not really important—the fun is in the doing and the learning. For the same reasons, a teacher should never hesitate to undertake cooking experiences because of her own lack of knowledge. Knowledge expands with practice for both teachers and children.

Do not display your own dislikes or prejudices about food in front of the children. They, like your enthusiasms, will communicate themselves to the children if you allow them to. So be sure to plan experiences you feel comfortable with.

Let the parents share in the cooking activities whenever possible, either by inviting them to school or by having the children take foods they have made, home. Very often this is the first time a parent becomes aware that such young children can do any cooking on their own. You might also encourage the children to volunteer to help cook at home. And you might provide an assortment of pots, pans, utensils, dishes, dishpans, and the like in the play area of your nursery school, so the children can use them in dramatic play.

Whenever possible, arrange field trips to dairies, farms, hatcheries, bakeries, candy factories, canneries, or other places where food is produced. This will help the children become aware of where the foods they eat come from and how they are prepared. They should also have some opportunities to shop for foods they will be preparing. On shopping trips they see what is available, they help make choices, and they learn to use scales and to compare prices.

Basic Techniques

Preparation and Preplanning

Check your equipment against the recipe you plan to follow, to see whether you have to borrow anything. Then make a written shopping list for ingredients you don't have on hand. On the day of the lesson, get all the food and equipment out of storage before you begin. (It can be handy to have a tray or two to put them all on.)

Demonstration

In the beginning it is advisable to demonstrate such techniques as cutting, measuring, and mixing, and it can be good to repeat those demonstrations from time to time. Allow one of the more capable children to demonstrate, whenever you can.

Visual Aids

Children are very visually-oriented. Photographs in magazines, books, and encyclopedias, as well as posters from fruit and vegetable companies can reinforce learning immediately and later, after some time has passed. Filmstrips can be bought or made (by drawing on blank film). Field trips to a library to find books with the names and pictures of unknown foods can be interesting and informative to children. Food magazines can be a valuable source of pictures of fruits and vegetables that do not grow in your area. Further sources of enrichment materials are listed on p. 163.

Working with Other Senses

Tasting, feeling, and smelling are also very interesting to children, so incorporate them throughout your cooking lessons. Remember to allow time for each child to touch, taste, and smell each ingredient during the lesson, in addition to eating the finished product.

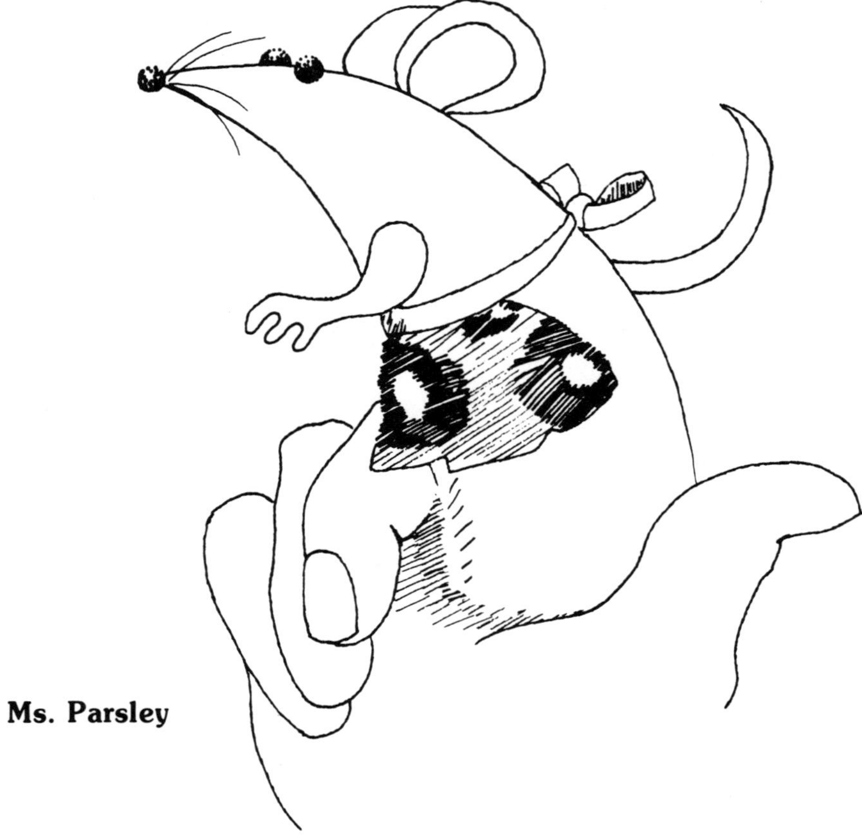

Ms. Parsley

Cut the pieces out of felt, sew a
seam up the back and down the
front of the body and turn it
right-side-out, and then sew the
tail, arms, ears, eyes, and nose to
the body. Use beads for the two eyes
and the nose. The whiskers can
be made of straw. If you wish, make
an apron of small-print cotton with
a ribbon for a waistband and ties.

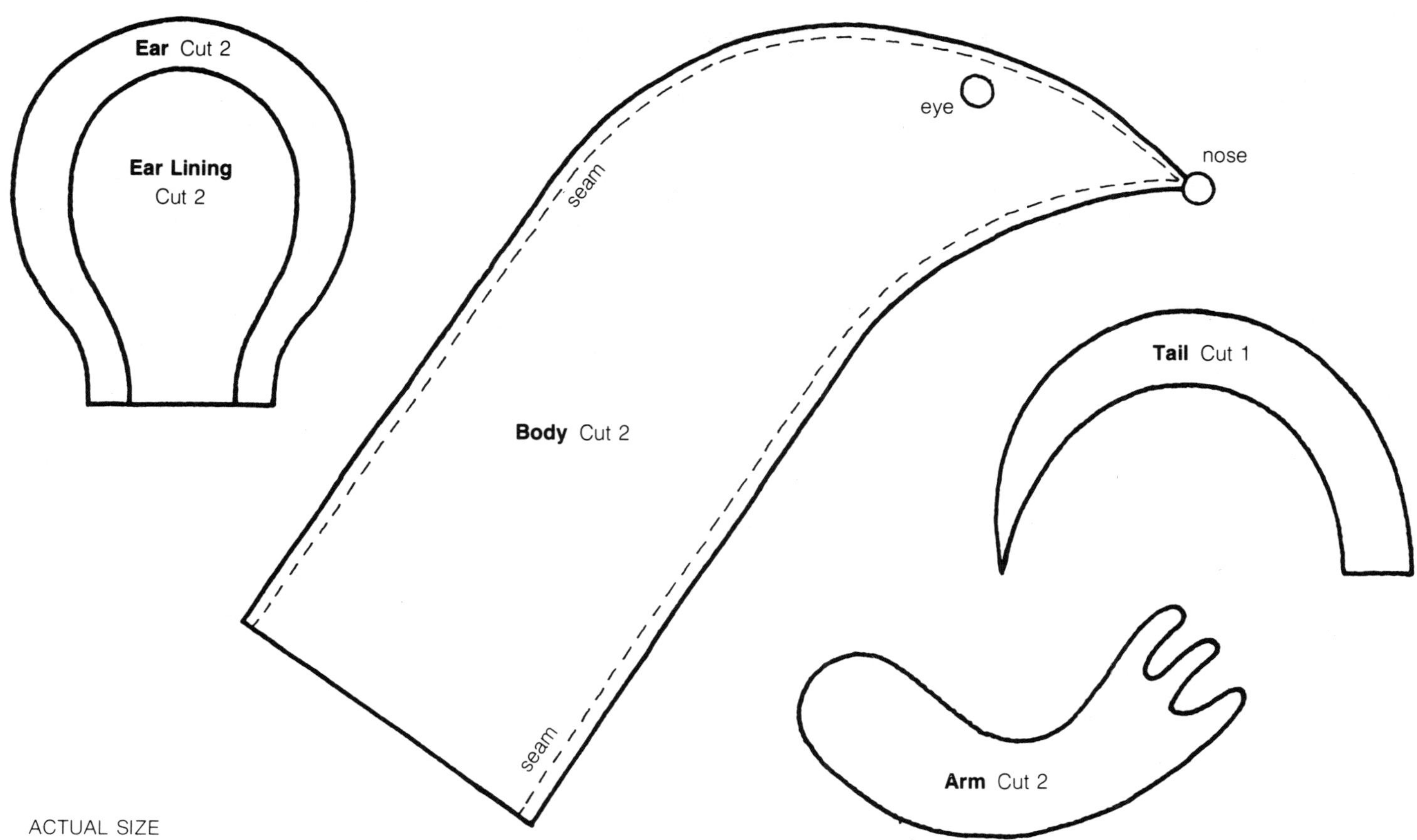

Ear Cut 2
Ear Lining Cut 2
eye
nose
seam
Body Cut 2
seam
Tail Cut 1
Arm Cut 2
ACTUAL SIZE

Remember to include learning about such areas as science, mathematics, nature, farming, and marketing in your cooking lessons wherever they are appropriate. We have suggested some possibilities for enrichment with our recipes, but creative teachers will be able to carry those ideas further. For example, if there is a child in the class whose parents will contribute some special ethnic cooking, take advantage of that bonus resource. You might even enhance the experience by showing pictures of where the special foods come from, what the people wear there, and the land, or by teaching the children songs or dances from that culture. Not only are such experiences enjoyable for the class, but they make the children who contribute very proud of their parents and themselves for sharing things that are part of their special backgrounds. Holidays and festivals present unlimited opportunities for similar broadening of the children's cultural and gastronomic experience.

Puppetry and Patterns*

As a teaching aid or an attention-holder, the dramatic appeal of the lively and amusing puppet has no equal. We have often seen that children retain what they have learned with the help of a puppet more distinctly than what they have heard or seen demonstrated by a mere human being.

The simplicity with which the two puppets Ms. Parsley and Mr. Hush Puppy are designed places them within range of even the youngest or least experienced puppeteer, to make or to manipulate. Nursery-school teachers might encourage children to create their own versions of these puppets by copying the patterns for the children to take home so that, with parental assistance, they can make their own cooking helpers. Having their own puppets at home can help children remember cooking processes and information about nutrition to share with their families.

*For the Ms. Parsley and Mr. Hush Puppy patterns and for her generous help in writing this section on puppetry, we are indebted to puppeteer Betsy Brown of Los Angeles, California.

Using the puppets can also help teachers feel more confident and daring in the perhaps-new area of nutrition and cooking. Ms. Parsley (a finger puppet) and Mr. Hush Puppy (a hand puppet) can support the lessons by encouraging, by amusing, and by stimulating discussion. Movements as simple as dusting flour from a board or wiping up spilt milk or stirring batter in a mixing bowl can be appealing pantomimes. The puppets do not need to talk but can "whisper" in the teacher's ear, after which the teacher can explain, "Ms. Parsley wants to make cookies today," or whatever.

Ms. Parsley is especially good at directing activities and making suggestions, while Mr. Hush Puppy can actually demonstrate the use of equipment or handle visual aids. Measuring cups, spoons, and bowls Mr. Hush Puppy handles should be full-size, for small children gain confidence from seeing an even-smaller puppet hold a regular measuring cup or a large wooden spoon.

The two might "live" in two pockets of the teacher's cooking apron, and they might wear a bit of a costume for holiday or ethnic food lessons. Both can be operated by children as well as by the teacher. However they are used, the puppets can help make cooking and nutrition lessons great fun!

Equipment We have found it best to buy sturdy, well-made equipment—the best we could afford. This equipment should be used only for actual cooking experiences and should be stored in a special place, away from kitchen tools that are used for dramatic play. Remember to check it periodically, so you can discard pieces that no longer operate properly.

If you limit the number of children who participate in cooking lessons to no more than eight to twelve for one teacher, as suggested earlier, you need only a minimum of equipment. It is possible to purchase many of the things you need second-hand at salvage shops, junk stores, garage sales, second-hand stores, the resale shops of the Salvation Army and Goodwill Industries and others like them, school fairs, church bazaars, and such. And, though we

Mr. Hush Puppy

Soft textures add to Mr. Hush Puppy's appeal, so cut the body from corduroy or fur fabric. Cut the paws, the eyes, and the nose from felt, and attach them to the body with glue after the body has been sewn and turned right-side-out. Cut the ears from felt, and sew them to the head. Stuff the head with cotton batting or nylon stockings, and wind a rubber band around the neck two or three times. Make a small hem at the open end of the puppet. If you wish, you can make a chef's hat and apron from white felt. A full-size pattern, increased to scale, should measure 14 inches in length and about 7 inches from the tip of the paw to the fold.

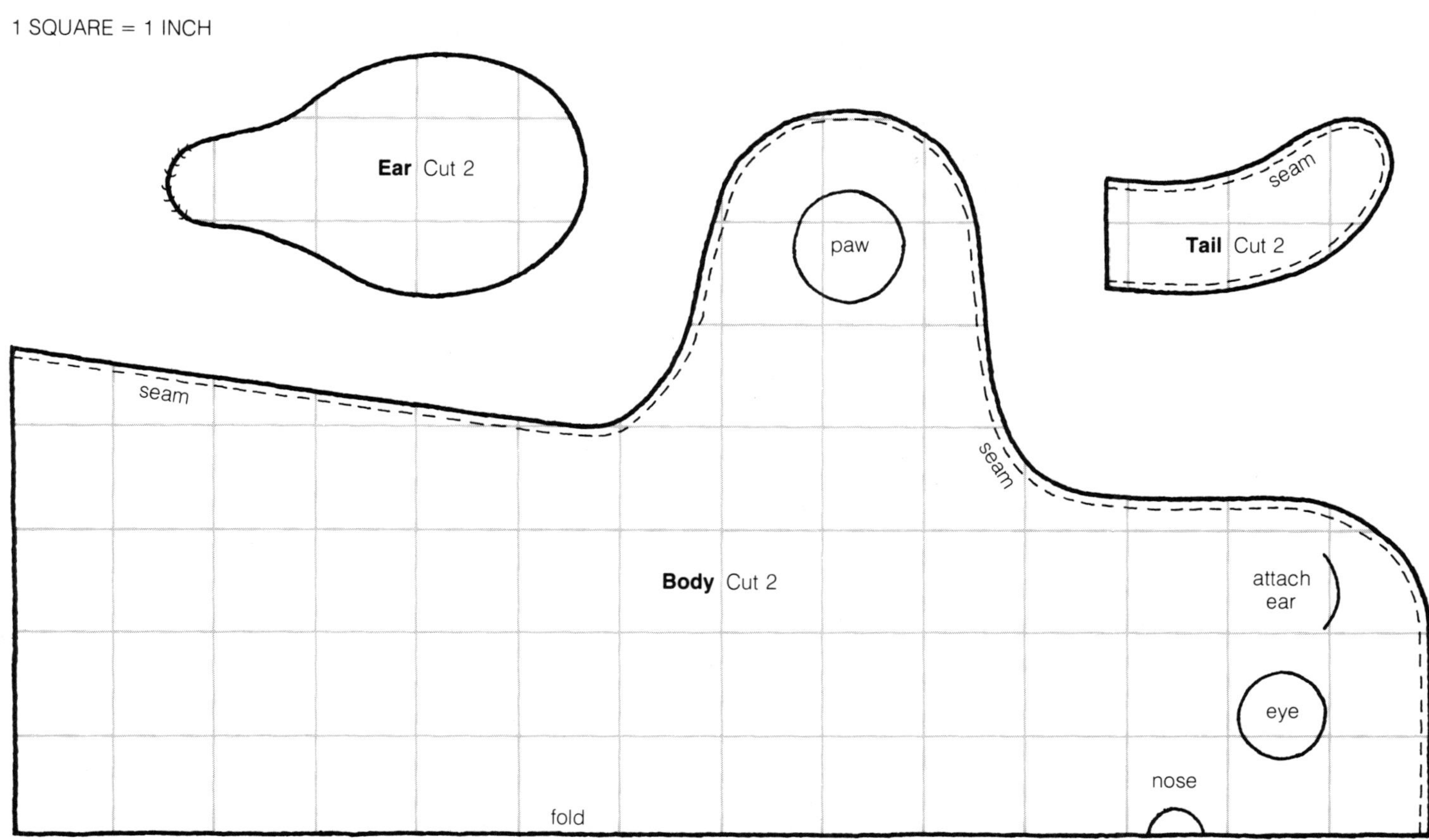

1 SQUARE = 1 INCH
Ear Cut 2
paw
seam
Tail Cut 2
seam
Body Cut 2
seam
attach ear
eye
nose
fold

believe schools are responsible for supplying the equipment for teaching, you can borrow or bring in special items in a pinch.

When the cost is low, you can provide duplicate equipment for each child, which allows active participation and cuts down on waiting.

We have found that toy-sized equipment is not always serviceable, but if you can find scaled-down pieces that work well, you might prefer to use them.

Basic Equipment

Rotary eggbeater
Hot plate with 1 or 2 burners
Electric skillet
Paring knife (sharp)
4 stainless steel or plastic mixing bowls of graduated sizes
Flour sifter
Biscuit and cookie cutters in many shapes
Pot holders
Large, two-tined fork
2 wooden mixing spoons
2 cookie sheets
Pyrex saucepan with lid (1½ quarts)
Rolling pin

Spatulas, short- and long-bladed
Pancake turners, short- and long-handled
An apron for each child, and a chef's hat if possible
Clock timer
Measuring spoons
Measuring cups (fractional for dry ingredients and Pyrex for liquids)
2 muffin tins (12 wells each)
Wooden cutting board
Rubber scraper
Clean-up equipment (dishpan, soap, washcloths, towels, drainer, sponge)
Cooling rack

Optional Equipment

Electric griddle
Corn popper
Pyrex custard cups (1 for each child)
Strainer

Tray, for holding food and equipment
Portable refrigerator
Blender

Measuring   Measuring may have become second nature to adults, but to young children it is a whole new world. The techniques that are involved give practice in large- and small-muscle development and in mathematics, as well as preparing the children for their cooking experiences. So measuring, by itself, makes a valid educational experience. Dry ingredients are best measured in fractional measuring cups, in which they can be leveled off with a spatula, whereas liquids are best measured in Pyrex or metal measuring cups.

Before starting the cooking lessons, teachers should acquaint themselves with the following common measurements and equivalents. Children can become familiar with them, too, with practice, though for some they may be too difficult.

A pinch = $\frac{1}{16}$ to $\frac{1}{8}$ tsp	2 cups = 1 pint
Teaspoon (tsp)	4 cups = 1 quart = 32 fluid ounces
Tablespoon (tbsp) = 3 tsp = $\frac{1}{2}$ ounce	4 quarts = 1 gallon
1 cup = 16 tbsp = 8 ounces	16 dry ounces = 1 pound
$\frac{1}{3}$ cup = $5\frac{1}{3}$ tbsp	4 sticks of butter = 1 pound
$\frac{1}{4}$ cup = 4 tbsp	1 stick of butter = $\frac{1}{2}$ cup

Two cups of most foods weigh 1 pound (you may remember the saying "a pint's a pound the world around"). But two notable exceptions are flour and powdered sugar, which are 4 cups to the pound.

Children should be encouraged to learn some of the more fundamental measurements, such as the following: teaspoon, tablespoon, $\frac{1}{4}$ cup, $\frac{1}{3}$ cup, $\frac{1}{2}$ cup, 1 cup, 1 quart, and 1 gallon. Two- and three-year-olds can learn the terms; four- and five-year-olds can learn the terms, identify the utensils, and recognize the actual quantities.

When following a recipe, it may be a good idea for teachers to premeasure the ingredients in the kitchen before the lesson starts, and then have the children measure them again at the table as the recipe directs. This assures greater accuracy and will minimize clutter.

Experiments with Measuring

- Let the children fill Pyrex measuring cups with water and show them how to read liquid measurements at eye level. (Place the cups on the table for this.) Encourage them to guess out loud what various amounts of water will measure.
- Demonstrate how to fill measuring spoons with flour and level the flour off with the edge of a knife or spatula, catching the extra on a sheet of wax paper. Let the children practice this.
- Demonstrate how fractions of cups or tablespoons and teaspoons add up to whole cups. For example, pour four quarter-cups into a full cup. Be sure to count out loud and encourage the children to count with you. Also try pouring from larger measures into smaller ones.
- Measure out various foods, and weigh them on a scale. Compare sizes and weights. Encourage the children to make guesses about which weigh more. Weighing cotton batting makes a very interesting experiment.
- Sift flour onto wax paper. Pile it lightly into a fractional measuring cup. Level it off with the edge of a spatula or knife. Weigh it, and compare the weight with the weight of the same volume of unsifted flour.
- Shortening can be measured by water displacement. Put ½ cup water in a glass measuring cup, and add enough shortening to bring the level of water to the 1-cup mark. Be sure all the shortening is covered by water. Explain to the children that the water shows that you have ½ cup of shortening. If the children can do it, let them try it.

  Shortening can also be measured by packing into fractional measuring cups, and leveling it off with the edge of a spatula. The children are most interested to discover that shortening measured by displacement equals the amount measured in a ½-cup container by the second method (if done properly). The most effective way of showing this is to remove the shortening from the 1-cup glass measuring cup and show how it fills the ½-cup measuring cup exactly.

- Weigh out a pound each of popular foods like water, milk, rice, sugar, cereal, and powdered sugar. Then measure them. If the class wishes, let them make a chart of weights and measures and illustrate it.

Safety Safety is an important part of cooking that teachers must reinforce continually. You cannot assume that the children will remember your safety rules, so repeat them with each cooking experience, and be very conscious of safety yourself at all times.

The size of the group that is cooking is one factor. A teacher should only work with eight children at a time, or with ten or twelve if they are older, and if there is an assistant teacher. (Individual teachers will know how many they can handle.) If a group is too large, children will have to wait too long for their turns unless there is enough equipment for everyone. It is also safest for the children to wait in their seats for their turns if they are working at a table.

If you plan to use the school kitchen for cooking rather than setting up lessons in the classroom, please check with your local Health Department to see whether there are regulations about having children in nursery-school kitchens (or in public kitchens). It is also necessary to make arrangements ahead of time for removing children who misbehave during cooking lessons.

Use good, sturdy equipment, to minimize breakage and faulty operation. It is wise to give a short demonstration on using each piece of equipment before each lesson. Remove from use any chipped or cracked dishes, bowls, or enamel pots because of the danger of bacterial contamination, and explain to the children.

Heat Instruct the children right away about using electricity and burners, and show them what parts of each piece of equipment will get hot. Always use pot holders when handling hot food and equipment. And be on guard against letting the handles of pots and pans protrude over the edges of tables or the range, as they can be bumped and the contents spilled on someone. Do not let pot handles extend over other burners *at any time*, whether those burners are turned on or off.

Obviously, knives are dangerous for children to use. Nevertheless, that does not mean children cannot use knives or other sharp tools under the proper conditions. First you must let them know that playing with knives is strictly forbidden. Knives are not toys. Our recommendations for working with knives are as follows: (1) We suggest a minimum age of three years. With younger children, teachers may find it more satisfactory to cut up the ingredients ahead of time. (2) Knives should be small, for easy handling. (3) Knives should be kept sharp, as dull knives require you to press too hard on them, so they are likely to slip out of your hand readily. (4) Always use a wooden cutting board when slicing, cutting, or chopping. And be sure to clean it thoroughly after you are through, to keep bacteria from growing, which could contaminate the food you cut on it another time. (5) Never put knives into the dishwater with other utensils, and never allow them to remain in a dishpan filled with soapy water, partly because they may rust, but mainly because of the danger of cutting yourself or the children.

Electrical Appliances

When you use electrical equipment, double-check it for frayed cords and broken plugs each time. Do not use disabled equipment until it is properly repaired. Make sure the children are aware of where any electric cords are so they won't trip. Always disconnect appliances by pulling the plug out at the outlet, never by tugging on the cord.

Fire

Before your first cooking lesson, locate the fire extinguisher and know how to use it. If there isn't one and you have a small fire, quickly cover the fire with the lid of a pot or else dump baking soda on the fire to put it out by eliminating its supply of oxygen. If the fire is in the electrical wiring, turn off the switch and disconnect the appliance immediately. Never put any water on an electrical fire or a grease fire, as that will spread the flames and create steam.

First Aid

If a child does get burned, immediately immerse the burn in cold water or ice water until the pain subsides. Then bandage the burn loosely to guard against infection, which is the real danger of a burn. Under *no* condition should you put grease, butter, or other medication on burns.

(This could interfere with any necessary medical care.) Inform the parents in case they should think medical attention is called for.

If a child cuts himself or herself, wipe the injured area with liquid tincture of green soap or with plain soap and water. Bandage or apply a Band-Aid. (This not only keeps the wound clean, but it makes the child feel important.)

Follow the regular procedure of your nursery school regarding accidents when anything like this happens. Usually that includes notifying the parents immediately if it is serious or at the end of the day if it does not require their immediate attention. If you must call parents, be as calm as possible when you tell them about an injury, because their natural reaction is to be overly apprehensive.

Cleanliness

Before starting a cooking lesson, have all children wash their hands thoroughly with soap and water. Children are fascinated with the germs they cannot see, so they cooperate with this happily, especially when the teacher joins them. If a microscope is available, you might show them what is in their ordinary tap water (the germs are alive and move).

A demonstration of good dishwashing techniques is important early in your cooking program, whether or not dishwashing will be a regular part of your lessons. However, if time permits, we suggest that it be a part of your routine, for two reasons: (1) to emphasize the need to use hot, soapy water and to rinse well, for reasons of sanitation, and (2) to reinforce their learning to be responsible for cleaning up after themselves. You can have the children carry over the dishwashing techniques they learn into their dramatic play, as they enjoy the actual washing, rinsing, and drying of the dishes they use in the housekeeping area.

It is the teacher's responsibility to see that the area used for cooking experiences is left neat and clean after each session, but the children should be encouraged to help whenever possible. At the same time, teachers can make children aware of other cleanup duties, such as wiping off the refrigerator, the range, the counter tops, and the floor. (Naturally, all of this depends on your layout and legal restrictions.)

  If your Health Department does not permit children to go into the school kitchen, you can bring all the equipment to the table, where it will be at the proper height for children to use. Let each child perform one simple step, rotating jobs so everyone has a turn.

1. Start with two dishpans, one filled with comfortably hot, soapy water, and the other with clear, hot water for rinsing.
2. Show the children how to scrape the excess food off the dishes into a disposable bag with a plastic scraper.
3. Then stack and sort the glassware, silver, dishes, and pots and pans, to teach them how to organize. Tell them you will want to wash the least soiled dishes first, and proceed to the most soiled last so the water will stay clean as long as possible.
4. For washing the dishes use a small dishcloth or a piece of nylon net the children can handle easily. Make sure each dish is clean before the children go to the next step.
5. For thorough rinsing, let the child dip the dish into clear water several times. It is most convenient to stack and drain the clean dishes in a dish rack, but they can be laid on a clean towel, instead.
6. Let the children dry the dishes with clean, absorbent towels, and then if possible have them put the equipment and supplies away.

Of course, many schools use disposable mouth utensils (paper plates and cups and plastic forks and spoons), in which case the cleanup is considerably simplified.

2

Nutrition and Health

WHAT PRESCHOOLERS CAN LEARN AND HOW TO TEACH IT

The importance of the early association of food with love and security, although it is well known, is too often forgotten in the development of nursery-school curriculums. Good nutrition, happy meals and snack times, and the inclusion of food preparation and nutrition education in their programs are all positive ways in which nursery schools can make important contributions to their children's welfare and growth, as well as their social and emotional development.

Not nearly enough has been said or written about the part preschool teachers can play in helping to promote better health and nutrition for the children in their care. With the current trend toward extended day care—with individual children spending more hours a week in preschools and with children from a wider range of social and economic groups participating in day-care programs—teachers could have an increasing influence in that area.

In evaluating the health and nutrition of each child in a class, teachers might ask themselves these questions: (1) Is the child reasonably free from disease and infections? (2) Is the child growing bigger and stronger? (3) Does the child look good? *Note whether the child has healthy hair, good clear skin, clear alert eyes, a reasonable covering of fat in relation to bone structure, good appetite, and enough energy to get through the day.* (4) Does the child seem to have good emotional health? *Note whether the child thinks he or she is worthwhile and deserving, though small; whether the child relates to other children as well as to adults; whether the child feels loved and is able to love in return; whether the child is willing to do things for himself or herself and yet can ask for help when it's needed; whether the child is willing to participate in activities; and whether the child shows signs of a growing independence.*

Such questions can help teachers evaluate the pattern of a child's development within the context of the child's individual genetic makeup. This evaluation can help teachers work most beneficially with parents in identifying any problems that may exist, so they can seek professional help if it is needed. When problems are suspected, professional help should, of course, be sought.

Teaching Nutrition in the Preschool

Nutrition is probably best taught at the preschool level by using the Basic Four Food Groups Plan (see p. 25). This is a very simple classification of foods, a description of their nutrient content, and a scheme for combining them to achieve good nutrition (making allowances for the system's limitations). The plan is intended, of course, for normally healthy children and does not take account of special needs. Although the plan does have limitations, nevertheless it can be used effectively in the nursery school because of its simplicity and its familiarity to many parents. With frequent repetition and daily practice in applying the plan, young children can learn which foods are in each group, what nutrients they contain, and how to combine them for good nutrition.

It may be a little overwhelming to hear a three-year-old say there is protein in eggs and we need protein every day to grow, but this is what has convinced us that effective nutrition education can be started in early childhood. The serious nutritional problems encountered throughout this country at all economic levels have persuaded us that it is necessary.

Nutrients (what our bodies need)

The body needs carbohydrates, fats, proteins, minerals, vitamins, and water in order to function properly. The following is a simplified description of these required substances, or *nutrients*, as they are properly called. This review is primarily for teachers, but young children can learn to use the vocabulary and the information in the discussions that accompany their cooking lessons.

Carbohydrates (sugars and starches)

Function to furnish energy.

Food sources sugars, syrups, molasses, fruit, pasta, flour and flour products such as bread and rolls, cookies, crackers, cakes, and pies and pastries, in gelatin desserts and puddings, cereals, corn, potatoes and other starchy root vegetables, legumes, jams, jellies, soft drinks, candy, doughnuts, honey.

Fats (fats and oils, both obvious and hidden)

Function to furnish energy and carry fat-soluble vitamins (A, D, E, and K).

Food sources butter; lard; hydrogenated fats such as Crisco and Spry; margarine; meat fats; vegetable oils; cream; nuts; cheese; and the hidden fats in cakes, pies, cookies, candy, and fried foods.

Proteins (milk, fish, meat, poultry, eggs, cheese, soybeans)

Function to build and repair body tissues and to furnish energy.

Food sources meat, poultry, fish, milk, cheese, legumes (peas and beans), eggs, nuts, and whole-grain cereals.

Minerals   (calcium, iodine, iron, phosphorous, and about ten others)

FUNCTIONS calcium builds bones and teeth; iodine promotes the functioning of the thyroid gland, which affects mental and physical development by controlling the rate the tissue cells use oxygen; iron builds red blood cells; phosphorous builds bones and teeth. (These are probably the most important minerals to stress because they are lacking in many diets.)

FOOD SOURCES

Calcium milk, buttermilk, cheese, leafy green vegetables, soybeans, blackstrap molasses.

Iodine salt-water fish and iodized salt (iodized salt is best for daily use).

Iron meats (especially kidney and liver), eggs, apricots, dried fruit, green vegetables, fish, poultry, whole grains, oysters, yeast, and molasses. (Enriched flour is the best substitute for whole-wheat flour if that is not preferred.)

Phosphorous meats (especially liver), fish, poultry, yeast, yogurt, milk, cheese, whole-grain cereals, eggs, and legumes.

Vitamins   (A, B complex—the most important B vitamins to talk about are thiamine, or B_1, riboflavin, or B_2, and niacin, because these are lacking in many diets—C, D, E, and K)

FOOD SOURCES

Vitamin A fish-liver oil, liver, kidney, carrots, apricots, yams, green and yellow vegetables, butter, cream, whole milk, whole-milk cheeses, and egg yolks.

Vitamin B_1, thiamine meats, green vegetables, whole-wheat or enriched bread and flour, eggs, and legumes.

Vitamin B_2, riboflavin meats, eggs, milk, legumes, and green vegetables.

Vitamin B, niacin meat, eggs, legumes, whole-wheat or enriched flour, and bread.

Vitamin C fresh fruit (especially pineapple, apple, melons, and citrus fruits), berries, and raw vegetables.

Vitamin D fish-liver oil, liver, butter, eggs, and Vitamin D-fortified milk.
Vitamin E whole-grain cereals, fruits, and vegetables.
Vitamin K green leafy vegetables and whole-grain cereals.

Water Water is also considered a nutrient because of its importance to good health and nutrition. In addition to the water we drink as such, water is supplied to the body in other beverages, in soups, and in many other foods. (In school, children should be encouraged to drink as much water as they need.)

All of these nutrients, as well as others we haven't mentioned (for simplicity's sake), can be incorporated in the diet by following a system such as the Basic Four Food Groups Plan.

Limitations of the Plan The Basic Four Food Groups Plan (see p. 25) is just a simple way of classifying the foods we eat, so we can develop a guide for planning balanced meals. One of the limitations of this grouping is that it omits butter and other fats. The assumption is that fats are included in most American diets, anyway. This is probably so. Another limitation is that not all foods in each group contain the same nutrients and in similar quantities, so sometimes foods within a single group are not really interchangeable. This is particularly true of fruits and vegetables. Not all fruits and vegetables, for example, are good sources of Vitamin A and Vitamin C. Further, some trace minerals, such as zinc and magnesium, are also essential for good nutrition, but their presence in foods is so small that they are difficult to detect and they are often lost in processing. And there may even be other nutrients in food that haven't been identified so far. Because of these omissions, then, it is important to stress to the children that they need to eat a variety of foods within each food group.

The plan also neglects to mention the value of eating moderately, although it does suggest how many helpings of various foods to eat daily. Too much of some vitamins (A and D) and minerals can actually be toxic, just as too little can cause nutritional deficiencies and malnutrition. Just plain too much food can be unhealthy, as well. One of the greatest problems in health and nutrition in the United States today is our high-calorie diet, which causes considerable overweight. It is estimated that one in five Americans (children and adults) is overweight. Teachers should remember that the overweight child usually becomes an overweight adult. So, much can be done to prevent future problems by an alert and interested teacher, who helps children become aware of which foods to emphasize and which ones to go easy on for good health.

It is important to remember also that no one miracle food can bring about health, beauty, vitality, or eternal youth. Rather, it is a combination of foods, as suggested by the Four Food Groups Plan (compensating for its limitations) that can effectively promote good health. True, weight for weight, some foods do have more nutrients than others and should therefore be eaten more frequently. As an obvious example, a glass of milk has far more nutrients than a glass of soda pop. Young children can learn about foods with "empty calories" (fats or carbohydrates with few or no other nutrients, such as the soda pop, which contributes only the calories in the approximately 6 teaspoons of sugar in each 12-ounce glass) and compare them to foods with "armored calories" (such as the milk, which contains protein, vitamins, and minerals in addition to its calories). And they can thus learn not to fill up on empty calories. But even milk, which is considered an almost perfect food, is lacking in iron and Vitamin C—two of the vital nutrients—and could not alone provide good nutrition over any length of time. It is therefore even possible to consume too much milk.

Fads promoting certain foods or combinations of foods as having miraculous health-giving properties are common. But we firmly believe that in the long run it is the varied combinations of such systems as the Basic Four Food Groups Plan that can accomplish the goal of good nutrition.

The Basic Four Food Groups Plan

Good nutrition for children does not differ essentially from good nutrition for adults except in quantity. Each child's food intake should include foods from each of the following food groups daily—and at every meal, if possible—in the quantities suggested (see also Table 1, p. 33). Each food group is broad enough to allow for flexibility and variety of choice.

In studying the plan, it is easiest for young children to learn the names of the food groups first, then to learn several foods that belong in each group, and then to learn what nutrients the foods contain. Later they can try planning attractive meals containing foods from all groups.

Milk Group*

(milk and milk products)

RECOMMENDED QUANTITY 2 or 3 cups a day, or the equivalent.

NUTRITIONAL CONTRIBUTIONS

*Complete protein,*** for muscle and tissue growth and repair.
Calcium, to build bones and teeth.
Vitamin A, Vitamin B complex, and Vitamin D, for general health, growth, and development.
Calories, for activity and vitality.

Young children prefer their milk chilled. They enjoy pouring it from small, stable pitchers and drinking it through colored straws on occasion. When you cook milk and cheese, use low or moderate temperatures for maximum retention of flavor and nutrients. (This is true for all protein foods.)

---

*Recipes are in Chapters 3 and 4.
**Complete proteins contain all essential amino acids.

In order to increase milk consumption or to provide variety, milk may also be included in the diet in the following ways: Pour it on cereals, instead of cream. Cook hot cereals in milk instead of water. Serve milk desserts such as bread pudding, rice pudding, tapioca pudding, rennet dessert, and custards. Milk and cream soups are popular with children. And ice-cream, though it is not a true substitute for milk as it does contain a large amount of sugar, neverthe-less is superior to other snack foods such as candy, soda pop, cake, or pie.

Skim milk, and buttermilk, yogurt, and chocolate drink (which is made from skim milk) do have fewer calories than whole milk, but they lack a good deal of the Vitamin A that is normally dissolved in the milk fat. The same is true of cottage cheese, ricotta cheese, farmer cheese, and hoop cheese, all of which are usually made of skim milk. If skim-milk products are used extensively in a child's diet, the child may actually be deficient in Vitamin A. The consumption of skim milk may, however, be recommended for overweight children, with the Vitamin A deficiency being corrected by adding green and yellow vegetables to their diets in substantial amounts. (Those vegetables are good sources of carotene, which is changed to Vitamin A in the body.) Cream is less valuable than milk nutritionally because it is mostly fat and lacks most of the proteins, vitamins, and minerals of milk.

Kitchen Puppets

Cheese made from whole milk is an acceptable substitute for milk. About a 1¼-inch cube of such cheese is nutritionally equivalent to 8 ounces of milk. Children like such mild cheeses as cheddar, American, Swiss, and Monterey Jack. Cheese makes an excellent finger food in bite-size pieces. Cheese on crackers or bread (enriched or whole-wheat) is also popular with children. Cheese sauce on vegetables, fish, spaghetti, or macaroni is another tried-and-true favorite. The flavor of cottage cheese is also well liked by children, and its versatility makes it most useful. About ¾ cup is equivalent nutritionally to 8 ounces of skim milk. Plain yogurt mixed with fresh, frozen, or canned fruit is a refreshing snack or dessert.

*Meat Group** (meat, fish, poultry, eggs, legumes, and nuts)

RECOMMENDED QUANTITY two or three 2-ounce servings daily.

NUTRITIONAL CONTRIBUTIONS
*Complete protein,*** for muscle and tissue growth and development.
Vitamin B (thiamine, niacin, and others), to promote growth and general health.
Iron, to build red blood cells.
Calories, for energy and vitality.

Encourage children to eat one egg a day, if possible (fresh eggs taste best). It is unfortunate that eggs have been maligned for their high cholesterol content. They do have cholesterol, but when you think of the egg's excellent nutrient content and its comparatively small size, the concern about cholesterol does not seem so important, especially if the total diet is well balanced and moderate.

---

*Recipes are in Chapters 3 and 4.
**Complete proteins contain all essential amino acids.

Eggs should be stored in their original cartons in the refrigerator with the blunt ends up (the cartons help prevent the evaporation of moisture through the shells). They keep about a week. Like other protein foods, they become tough and rubbery when they are cooked improperly. They should always be cooked at low or moderate temperatures—definitely below boiling. Eggs are one food children can easily learn to cook for themselves—a hard-cooked egg, for example, is fun to peel and can be eaten by hand for an excellent snack. If children do not like eggs, they can be included in the diet in many ways—in puddings, custards, meat loaf, sauces, casseroles, and baking, to name a few.

Children especially love ground meat and hot dogs, so these foods can be served often. Fish, poultry, and other forms of meat are also enjoyed. Small pieces of cooked meat or chicken, perhaps on toothpicks, make excellent snacks. Meat, fish, and poultry, like eggs, should be cooked at low or moderate temperatures. High temperatures cause them to dry out, to lose flavor, and to toughen, as well as to lose nutrients.

The quality of the protein in legumes (peas and beans) and nuts is not as good as that in the other foods in this group. If legumes and nuts are used extensively in the diet, they should be combined often with meat, poultry, eggs, fish, or cheese, to improve their nutritional value. One advantage of these foods is their economy.

*Fruits and Vegetables Group** (all fruits and vegetables)

RECOMMENDED QUANTITY Four or five 2-ounce servings daily, including 1 serving of citrus fruit or the equivalent in Vitamin C** and 1 serving of a green or yellow vegetable or fruit for Vitamin A.

---

*Recipes are in Chapters 3 and 4.
**Foods that are equivalent to citrus fruit in Vitamin C include cabbage, green pepper, melon, and strawberry.

Vitamins and minerals, to build bones, teeth, blood, and tissues and to help promote growth and proper development.

Cellulose, or roughage, to help promote elimination.

Calories, to provide energy and vitality, although many fruits and vegetables are lower in calories than other foods.

Raw fruits and vegetables make excellent snacks (Vitamin C is easily destroyed in cooking). Allow children to eat fruits instead of vegetables when they are in periods of preferring fruits. Making an issue of any food dislike is very poor practice—a substitute can usually be found.

The best way of encouraging children to eat more fruits and vegetables is by example. Children learn a great deal by imitating those they love. If the group sets a good example and the child wishes to be part of the group, the desire to do as the group does is very strong. Children often eat many foods at school because they see other children eating them. Preschool teachers can take advantage of this by encouraging them to try unfamiliar foods.

Many vegetables, such as cauliflower and broccoli, which are normally eaten cooked, might be more acceptable to children in the raw state. Be sure to wash the raw vegetables thoroughly and leave the skins on whenever possible.

Try to help children become accustomed to eating cooked vegetables cooked only to the crisp state. They are more flavorful and have more nutrients and better color then than when they are more cooked and mushy.

When buying canned fruits, choose the light-syrup pack rather than the heavy-syrup pack. Dried fruits also make excellent snacks or desserts.

Children's tastes do change and develop. It is a good idea to offer children a fruit or vegetable they have disliked before, after a lapse of time. It is very possible for children to start liking foods at the second, third, or even the fourth exposure.

(breads, cereals, and pasta)

RECOMMENDED QUANTITY At least 1 child-size serving at each meal (¼ cup cooked cereal, ½ cup dry cereal, or ½ slice bread).

NUTRITIONAL CONTRIBUTIONS

Carbohydrates, to supply fuel for activity and vitality.
Vitamin B complex, small amounts, to promote health, growth, and development.
Iron, a small amount, to build red blood cells.
Roughage, in whole grains, to promote elimination.
Calories, to provide energy.

Whole-grain cereals like whole wheat, brown rice, oats, barley, and corn are more nutritious than refined cereals because of the vitamins and minerals they contain. If whole-grain cereals are rejected for some valid reason, then try using enriched or fortified cereals. Most ready-to-eat, or dry, cereals are at the bottom of the nutritional list. Unfortunately, they are all too popular with children. Eating such cereals with milk instead of cream and with fruits, honey, or brown sugar in small quantities will enhance their nutritional value. Maybe the study of good nutrition will help children change their preferences to the more nutritious cooked whole-grain cereals or Granola-type cereals.

Buttered bread with some kind of protein, like peanut butter or cheese, makes excellent snacks, which are even better when the children prepare them on their own. Children enjoy toasted bread and open-face sandwiches, cut in halves or quarters so they can handle them easily. These pieces also make good "pushers" to help push food onto forks or spoons as the children are eating.

---

*Recipes are in Chapters 3 and 4.

Children also like such starches as rice, spaghetti, and macaroni. When combined with milk, eggs, cheese, meats, fish, poultry, fruits, and vegetables to enrich them nutritionally, they have a valid place in the diet.

Butter and Other Fats   (not one of the four groups, but essential)

RECOMMENDED QUANTITY small amounts at each meal.

NUTRITIONAL CONTRIBUTIONS

Vitamin A, to promote general health, good vision, growth, and development.
Calories, for energy and vitality.

Since children may suffer Vitamin A deficiency to some degree, they should eat a small quantity of butter or fortified margarine at every meal. One-half tsp can, for example, be spread on ½ slice bread or be melted on cooked vegetables.

Although fats such as butter or fortified margarine are not a food group by themselves, they should not be ignored in planning for good nutrition. Other fats, oils, and hydrogenated fats contribute calories, but they are generally lacking in Vitamin A and should be eaten sparingly.

Combination Foods   Many dishes are combinations of foods in two or more groups. It is usually simple enough to analyze the contents of such a dish and assign the foods in it to their appropriate food groups. Even young children can learn to do this.

Applying the Plan   How can this information be used? Planning meals for children that are nutritionally balanced, and serving them attractively and in appropriate quantities are the next stage.

Children, parents, and teachers, after studying the Basic Four Food Groups Plan and its limitations, easily see how to combine foods for meals and snacks. The important first step in meal-planning is to review the goals. They are, in general, to plan meals that (1) are nutritionally adequate, (2) are attractive and tasty, (3) match the budget, (4) conform to individual preferences and traditions, and (5) are easy to prepare within the time, energy, and skill of the person who is to prepare them.

Meals traditionally follow patterns that young children can learn easily and then fill in with foods from each of the four food groups. Remind them to plan to use foods from each group at each meal if possible, and in the amounts per day recommended in Table 1 (p. 33).

Breakfast   The pattern for breakfast would be as follows:

- fruit or fruit juice, preferably citrus *(Fruits and Vegetables Group)*
- cereal *(Bread and Cereals Group)*
- egg or the equivalent *(Meat Group)*
- toast and butter *(Bread and Cereals Group and Fats)*
- beverage, preferably milk *(Milk Group)*

Using this pattern, breakfast can be planned for a week at a time (see Table 2, p. 41), giving attention to variety. For example, although citrus fruits are preferred because of their Vitamin C, other fruit juices or fruits (preferably fresh), can be served fairly often. Remember that it is nutritionally better to serve cooked cereals than dry cereals. And eating cereals with milk is preferable to taking them with cream because milk has more nutrients (cream is the fat without the protein, vitamins, and minerals of whole milk).

The protein portion of the meal—the egg or its equivalent—is very important. For children who don't like eggs, small servings of meat, fish, or poultry may be substituted. There is no law that says a child cannot have hamburger, cheese, or tuna fish for breakfast. One fact to remember is that bacon does not compare nutritionally with other meats. It can be served occasionally, however.

Table 1. Daily Food Intake Recommended for Preschoolers (average)

FOOD GROUP	NUMBER OF SERVINGS	SIZES OF SERVINGS
BREAD AND CEREALS (includes bread, cereals, rice, and pasta)	4 or more	½ to 1½ slices of bread, ½ to ¾ cup cooked cereal, cornmeal, macaroni, spaghetti, or rice
FRUITS AND VEGETABLES	1 of citrus fruit or other source of Vitamin C, such as tomato, cabbage, melon, or strawberry	½ cup, or a normal portion such as ½ to 1 medium-size orange or 4 ounces of juice
	1 of dark green or leafy vegetable or yellow fruit or vegetable for Vitamin A	2 to 4 tablespoonfuls
	at least 2 of other fruits and vegetables, cooked or raw	2 to 4 tablespoonfuls or a half or whole fruit or vegetable
MEAT (includes meat, poultry, fish, eggs, peas, beans, and nuts)	2 or more	2 to 4 tablespoonfuls (1 or 2 ounces), 1 egg, ½ cup cooked beans, 4 tbsp peanut butter
MILK (includes milk products)	2 or 3 cups (other dairy products may be substituted for milk)	½ to 1 cup milk, 1 ounce milk product

Toast, of course, can be replaced by bread, muffins, biscuits, or any other kind of bread-stuff (preferably made from whole-grain or enriched flours). Always use a small amount of butter or fortified margarine with the bread, to supply essential fat and Vitamin A.

All this breakfast is easy for the healthy child who has a good appetite to enjoy. But what about a child who often does not eat breakfast? This is worth serious discussion. Most children will not have eaten since the previous evening. If they don't eat breakfast, their blood sugar will probably drop quite low during the morning so that they may tire easily, behave badly, and lose their appetites for further meals. Therefore, teachers and parents must work to reeducate such children to change this habit.

Many don't eat breakfast because they are not given enough time to eat; others do not get enough sleep. Others are following poor examples set by members of their families. Sometimes if a mother will sit down with her child and make a social occasion of breakfast, the child will respond positively. Admittedly, this is extremely difficult for the working mother, but the results may surprise her if she can work out something of this nature. Children are also more inclined to eat if they learn to make their own simple breakfasts (with or without cooking).

What about the child who cannot eat much for breakfast? The easiest item to eliminate from the breakfast pattern is cereal because it makes the smallest nutritional contribution. Or perhaps giving children smaller quantities of each food will encourage them to eat. Other children might eat part of their breakfasts at home and take the rest to school. A peeled hard-cooked egg or a piece of cheese and a half piece of toast are easy to carry to school if that is absolutely necessary. Although it is really the responsibility of the parents to give the children breakfast, sometimes a school must make concessions like this for the welfare of a child.

For mothers who have too little time to prepare breakfast, instant cereal, frozen breakfasts, or instant breakfasts may be the answer, although they are not nearly as nutritious as less processed foods. Preparing breakfast the night before is another possibility. In any event, more attention should be paid to the problem. More children skip breakfast than many people realize, which may account for many of the problems young children have in making their adjustments to school. Hungry children cannot focus their attention on learning, so teachers would do well to educate both the children and the parents about the value of eating an adequate breakfast.

Snacks The snacks served in nursery schools should be considered carefully. Too many schools take the easy way out by serving commercial punch and cookies for snacks too often because they are easy and cheap. But that is nutritionally unacceptable. Snacks should meet part of the children's daily nutritional requirements. They should not be empty calories, but should usually contain some protein and a small amount of fat to sustain the children until their next meal. Cookies containing such ingredients as oatmeal, nuts, and peanut butter may be served with milk now and then, especially if the children have made the cookies. Some good possibilities for snacks are the following:

- graham crackers and milk
- 3 or 4 bite-size pieces of cheese, jerky, meat, and/or chicken on a toothpick with crackers or whole-wheat bread
- graham crackers, peanut butter, and fruit or vegetable juice
- bread, butter, and milk
- dried fruit and milk
- sliced egg, bread, crackers, and juice
- pudding or gelatin dessert
- applesauce and milk
- fresh fruit and milk
- sardines or tuna on crackers and juice
- raw vegetables and milk
- homemade milk shakes or fruit shakes
- nuts and fruit

Remember to serve snacks in small portions so the children are not overwhelmed, but always encourage them to have seconds. Children enjoy making snacks for themselves individually and for the class whenever either is possible.

Lunch and Dinner Lunch and dinner may be considered simultaneously, as the pattern for the two meals is the same:

- soup *(group varies)*
- salad *(Fruits and Vegetables Group)*
- starch *(Fruits and Vegetables Group or Bread and Cereals Group)*
- main dish *(Meat Group alone or combined with others)*
- vegetables, one or two *(Fruits and Vegetables Group)*
- bread *(Bread and Cereals Group)*
- butter *(Fats)*
- dessert *(Fruits and Vegetables Group or combinations of groups)*
- beverage (preferably *Milk Group*)

The above pattern does furnish foods from each of the four groups. But, again, many children will not be able to or want to eat this much at one meal. The least nutritious foods should be eliminated from the plan first, such as the soup, the starch, the bread, and perhaps the dessert, depending on what it is. Here also a child may be stimulated to eat a greater variety of foods if served very small portions.

Or, part of the meal may be eaten later as a snack. Many children and adults will eat more if they eat small amounts every two or three hours. Three meals a day is not the best pattern for everyone. Obviously, many small meals a day are not feasible for schools, but that pattern is valid for the parents of problem eaters to consider. Bedtime snacks are a matter of individual choice. For children who cannot eat much at dinner who are hungry at bedtime, light protein snacks are justifiable and may help them sleep better. Any of the snacks suggested above would be suitable, as would cooked cereal, eggnog, or any other simple food the children like. But they should not have empty calories.

Children should be allowed the dignity of individuality where choices of foods and patterns of eating are concerned, as far as is feasible for the parents and the schools they attend.

Making Meals Attractive

It has often been said that we eat with our eyes. This is especially true of children, who are generally very sensitive to their environments. The color of the foods on a plate makes a first powerful impact on a child. Bright colors that harmonize make a pleasing impression. Compare, for example, the appearance of a luncheon dish consisting of boiled white meat of chicken, mashed potatoes, and cauliflower served on a white plate, with the appearance of a luncheon dish consisting of roast chicken, baked potato, and broccoli on a tinted or patterned plate. Pleasing combinations of colors appeal to the eyes and stimulate appetites.

The careful use of color is almost as important in planning meals as are good nutrition and variety of tastes. An interesting combination of textures enhances a meal similarly. Too many soft textures at one meal are as undesirable as too many crisp textures. The shapes of the foods served should also be considered—generally they should vary. Hot foods should be served hot and cold foods, cold, with a range at each meal, for contrast and interest. However, children prefer their food not to be very hot. They do like cold drinks and ice-cream, but they usually eat them slowly, to adjust to the temperature.

Combinations of flavors are also important. Some traditional combinations like turkey and cranberry sauce can be overused, so it is fun to consider varying them from time to time. Too many strong flavors at one meal are undesirable, as they dull the taste buds by overstimulation. And too many bland flavors at the same meal are uninteresting. Too many sweet foods or too many sour foods can destroy the balance of flavors. Repetition of a flavor in more than one dish in a single meal, (for instance, tomato soup with tomato salad) is also considered poor planning.

The idea is to strive for balance and variety of color, texture, shape, temperature, and flavor. These principles apply to meal-planning for children, even though the meals children eat and cook are simple.

Well planned, nutritious meals need not be expensive. It is important to buy the best food you can afford that is clean, wholesome, and properly stored. Again, this need not be expensive. For example, the foods in the Bread and Cereals Group are usually the least expensive, and you can use small quantities of food from the Meat Group or the Milk Group to enhance their protein. Generally speaking, plant proteins like those in legumes, nuts, and cereals are lacking essential amino acids, so it is best to combine them with complete protein foods like meats, eggs, and cheeses. Thus, dishes like macaroni or noodles with meat or cheese; spaghetti with meatballs or meat sauce; beans with meatballs or frankfurters; and rice with cheese, chicken, or tuna are all nutritious as well as being popular with children.

Ground meat is well liked and is one of the least expensive meats. Tuna is also popular, as is chicken—both comparatively low in cost. Cottage cheese is well liked and inexpensive and can even be made by the children during a cooking lesson (see p. 69). American cheese or Monterey Jack cheese are also enjoyed by children, and, although they are somewhat expensive, they can go a long way because they are concentrated and have no waste. Fruits and vegetables are least expensive and most flavorful and nutritious when they are purchased in season. Skim-milk powder, although it is not the nutritional equivalent of whole milk, can be used in many ways much cheaper than fresh whole milk. Skim milk, however, is not generally recommended as a substitute beverage for whole milk for the average child. Rather, it is best used in cooking. Meat is the most expensive food, so you can cut costs by substituting poultry, fish, and egg dishes. (By the way, all cuts of meat—expensive or inexpensive—are nutritionally equal.)

Well advertised name-brand products are usually relatively expensive. Better buys can be the house brands of large markets. To be sure of costs, compute the unit prices of different sizes and brands of a food by dividing the number of ounces or pounds in each package into the total price and then comparing the cost per ounce or the cost per pound.

There are several drawbacks to buying wholesale for the small nursery school. If you buy too much more than you need at one time, you may tie up too much of your money in stock. Storage can be a problem, as well, as can spoilage and a lack of variety. But it can save money to buy in bulk such everyday staples as graham crackers, other crackers, rice, beans, tomato sauce, fruit juice, canned fruits and vegetables. A few days of cooking will give you an idea of what to buy and in what quantities.

Such convenience foods as prepared canned or frozen foods, although time-savers, are usually quite expensive, though there are occasional exceptions. A comparison of costs, keeping in mind the time and effort of preparation, will reveal the best choice.

Planning Menus Ahead

Planning is an essential part of a school cooking program. Planning on paper for several days at a time, or even for a week, allows you to pay proper attention to such concerns as nutritional balance, variety, and combinations of colors and flavors. A plan also gives you a chance to think in advance about the timing of the efforts involved in preparing each event. Shopping lists are easier to make when your plan is on paper. Remember, however, that any plan must be flexible enough to allow for last-minute changes because of sales, donations, and such. It has been our experience that making the first few plans is somewhat time-consuming, but after that it becomes easier, and is always worth the effort.

A sample preschool menu plan for a week of snacks and lunches appears in Table 2. Although the lunches may contain more variety than many schools might want to offer, this schedule has many advantages. The dishes are comparatively simple to prepare, and the cost is within the average nursery-school budget. (It should be repeated that the servings will be small because of the large variety of foods.) Most snacks here include some form of protein, and many of them can be made by the children. Menus should vary from week to week. Avoid the cliché of "Monday, spaghetti; Tuesday, baked beans . . ." in order to provide vital nutritional variation and to widen the children's experience with food.

No Two Are Exactly Alike

Each child, like each adult, is unique and should be allowed to grow and develop according to his or her individual pattern. Children must be properly nourished to fulfill their genetic potentials, but no amount of food can make them develop beyond their genetic limits or their inherited determination.

Children grow in spurts, during which they eat more food. When growth slows down, most children eat less. Development cannot be hurried. We can only supply the nutrients that are needed. Deprivation of nutrients at crucial stages not only impairs bodily growth, but hinders the development of internal organs and mental growth, as well. The particular tragedy is that once a crucial stage is past, there is no retracing to repair the damage caused by a lack of certain nutrients.

Along with our concern for the fulfillment of their potential for growth and development, we must allow children the privilege of being independent when they want to be. When they attempt to feed themselves, they should be allowed to, messy as the results may be.

Children react as differently to food as they do to other situations. Each one reacts in his or her own way. Some have especially strong reactions to some food. This individuality should be respected, within the limits of the environment.

Table 2. A Week's Menu of Snacks and Lunches for Preschools

	MONDAY	TUESDAY	WEDNESDAY	THURSDAY	FRIDAY
MORNING SNACK	graham crackers and milk	hard-cooked egg quarters and milk	raisins and milk	raw vegetables and milk	cheese bites on toothpicks and fresh fruit
LUNCH	meat loaf, baked potato, string beans, celery sticks, buttered whole-wheat bread, milk, custard	stewed chicken, rice pilaf, mixed vegetables, crackers, milk, fresh fruit	macaroni and cheese, tossed lettuce and tomato salad, broccoli, buttered rye bread, milk, applesauce, cookie	baked beans with hot dogs, spinach, carrot sticks, buttered raisin bread, milk, fruit gelatin	creamed tuna, mashed potatoes, green peas, buttered whole-wheat bread, milk, fresh fruit
AFTERNOON SNACK	fresh fruit and milk	cheese sandwiches and vegetable juice	fruit shake	fresh fruit slices with cottage cheese	Finger Jello and milk

All children go through periods of great activity. Sometimes eating then seems to be the least important part of their lives. Generally, the periods pass, as the children reach other stages of development. It is usually best to take such variations calmly.

Children sometimes have periods of contrariness. If a child refuses to eat, it is best to remove the food. Children should never get the idea that their refusal of food can cause emotional upheaval in others. One tried-and-true method is to offer problem eaters a choice of foods. Usually they will make a choice. Thus the children feel they are getting their own way, but they still are eating from among the foods offered. If the choices are of equal nutritional quality, nothing is lost.

Wanting to do what the rest of the group does can be a very great incentive to problem eaters. It is not uncommon to see such children forget their hang-ups about food when they see the rest of the children eating calmly and enjoying the whole social event with gusto. Nursery schools can offer children a unique opportunity to expand their horizons on food and to overcome poor food habits by watching other children. Teachers, however, should avoid calling attention to food habits by undue praise or criticism. Eating is a natural and normal activity in life. It should always be kept that way, in its normal perspective.

Expect some dawdling over meals and snacks. When the first pangs of hunger have been satisfied, children sometimes lose some of their interest in eating and may be in no hurry to continue at the pace adults wish. The child's concept of time is different. Allow a reasonable amount of time to eat (½ hour for lunch, 10 or 15 minutes for snacks), and then remove the plate. Be sure, however, that you do give enough time. Many nursery schools often do not allow long enough for eating or for other activities, which can create unnecessary tension in the children. Remember, also, to serve small quantities—a teaspoonful, if need be.

Children often go on jags when they favor a single food almost exclusively. Experience has shown that being casual and allowing the child to work it through usually is the best way to handle this. Giving in, within reason, doesn't spoil children, but allows them the dignity of individuality.

Experience has also proved that most children function both in school and at home with a few simple, reasonably consistent rules for eating, such as the following:

1. Clean hands before and after eating.
2. No playing with food.
3. No threatening, bribing, or pleading with children to eat.
4. After a reasonable time, food that hasn't been eaten is removed and forgotten.

This discussion applies to normally healthy children. The child who is sick or who has severe problems of one kind or another, obviously should have medical or other treatment and should follow the course prescribed.

Suggestions for Happy Eating

- Avoid conflict over food. A pleasant atmosphere is as important for healthy eating as is the proper food.
- Eating should be an enjoyable experience. A tired, upset child cannot enjoy eating, so getting ready to eat should be done in a relaxed way. If a child is upset, it may just be better to postpone eating for a while.
- Serve food attractively. The appearance of food is just as important to children as the flavor. They enjoy bright colors, attractive combinations of food, colorful dishes, cups, cloths, napkins, and decorations.
- Children prefer mild flavors, and most do not like strong-tasting food. Their taste buds have different levels of sensitivity than adults' do, so children often react differently to foods. Therefore, their preferences should be respected, within reason.
- Children usually prefer individual foods to be separated from each other on the plate.
- Servings that are too large can discourage appetites. Rather, children should be given small amounts and be encouraged to ask for second helpings, if they wish. This fosters decision-making and allows for individual freedom.

- When introducing an unfamiliar food, serve a small portion along with familiar foods. Discussion, interest, and enthusiasm about the new food may stimulate children to try it. If anyone is not interested, forget it, and try again with that child some other time.
- Dessert is an integral part of a meal. Foods that have vitamins and minerals in addition to calories are the best to use. The list of such desserts could include fruits (fresh, frozen, or canned—raw or cooked), custards, simple puddings, gelatin puddings, graham crackers with peanut butter, and the like. If children prefer to eat dessert with the rest of the meal, as some do, no real harm is done, but it should not be encouraged. And desserts should never be used as rewards for eating other foods. If desserts are considered part of the balanced meal, they no longer have glamour or unwarranted importance. Rich cakes, pies, pastries, sundaes, and the like are not recommended for children and should only be offered very rarely.
- Children should have freedom to eat in their own ways. Table manners may be encouraged after they have matured sufficiently to hold spoons. (It is important to choose small utensils children can handle easily.) When they are seated comfortably at the right height for them, and are helped to feel part of the group, it is easier for children to manage eating.
- Most children cannot eat enough at one meal to tide them over to the next. They have a small capacity and a high energy output. Without sufficient food, they can develop temporary hypoglycemia (low blood sugar), which can cause them fatigue, irritability, sleepiness, and depression, as well as shortening their attention spans. Many behavior problems may very well be caused by hypoglycemia. Therefore, snacks are advisable. Snacks should be eaten at regular times (midmorning and after afternoon naps) and should include part of the daily nutritional content, as outlined earlier. If any children wish to eat all day long, consider giving them more protein at meals or think about whether their eating is a symptom of boredom, insecurity, or loneliness.

Teaching Techniques   Because nutrition could be considered somewhat abstract, it is up to the teacher to make it real by applying it to the children's daily lives. In general, we suggest using a variety of techniques, such as the following:

- Ask direct questions.
- Have the children repeat the names of foods and facts after you.
- Tell stories about foods—especially ones involving the names of children who are present.
- Demonstrate, or have parents, other adults, or children demonstrate.
- Use illustrations—drawings, photographs, models, and the puppets described in Chapter 1—to make your points.
- Use music—make up words about nutrition to fit a favorite melody, as in the example below.

THE LITTLE LAMB'S NUTRITION SONG (Lyrics by Sybil Limon)

(To the tune of "Mary Had a Little Lamb")

Good nutrition makes you grow
From head to toe—yo, ho, ho!
But there are rules you have to know
To get your good nutrition.

Vegetables and fruits for you
Protein too—yoo, hoo, hoo!
Cereal or bread and milk
Will give you good nutrition.

Protein can be meat or fish
Or chicken dish—tish, tish, tish!
Cheese or eggs or beans or nuts
Will give you good nutrition.

Vegetables or fruits for snacks
And with meals—click, click, clack!
Eat them dried or cooked or raw
To get your good nutrition.

Review and Discussion

- Ask the children to name the foods they are eating.
- Have the children name the ingredients they think are in mixed dishes.
- Have the children name other dishes that have the same ingredients as the dish they are eating.
- Discuss with the children the sources of the foods they are eating.
- Let the children name and discuss what food groups the foods they are eating belong to.
- Have the children discuss what nutrients are in the foods they are eating.
- Let the children discuss how to combine foods they know or foods they've just met for a balanced meal.
- Have the children describe the patterns of breakfast, lunch, dinner, and snacks, and tell what they eat at home for those meals.
- Let the children tell the differences between what they eat at home and what they eat at school.
- Have them discuss the functions of the major nutrients.
- Let the children "teach" parents what good nutrition is.
- At lunch or at snack time, discuss colors, textures, tastes, and nutritional contributions of foods the children are eating. Some questions you might use to start a discussion are: What color are these carrot sticks? What is in the carrot sticks that is good for us? How does this carrot feel to you? How does the carrot taste?

Games and Activities

- *Blow-up balloons.* Insert a rolled-up picture of a food in a balloon. Then blow the balloon up. Give a child a pin with which to burst it. When the balloon bursts, encourage the children to describe the food in the picture, its contribution to good nutrition, its color, its texture, how to cook it, and so forth. Follow with a balloon for each child to burst in turn, with pictures of foods from each of the food groups.

- *Let's Have a Party*, or *Let's Go On a Picnic*. Ask questions like: What foods will we take? What nutrients do they contain? How do they help us to be healthy?
- *Fishing for the Four Food Groups*. For practice in learning the Basic Four Food Groups, make fishing poles out of 24-inch to 36-inch lengths of dowel. Tie on them, 12-inch pieces of string with magnets tied at the other ends. Scatter pictures of foods on the floor or table, each with a paper clip attached. Have the children "fish" for foods of each food group, and perhaps discuss what contribution each "fish" they catch makes to nutrition.
- *Flash Cards*. Paste pictures of foods on cards. Have one child hold the cards up to the group. Ask for the name of the food that is pictured, what food group it is in, and what its nutritional contribution is.
- *"I Went to the Kitchen."* Have the children take turns finishing brief stories beginning, "I went to the kitchen, and I . . . ." Older children can add items to a single story in turn.
- *Plate Stories*. Have a random collection of paper plates to paste pictures of foods on (one food each for younger children, complete meals for older). Let the children select their favorite foods, foods they may have cooked, or foods they would like to cook. Then have them tell, in turn, why those foods are good for us.
- *Cooking Lessons*. Discuss the nutrient contributions of the foods used in any of the cooking lessons and recipes.
- *Favorite Foods*. Have different children demonstrate how to make favorite foods if they can, or else bring them from home. Point out the nutrient contributions. Or invite a parent or another guest to demonstrate preparing a favorite food, and have the class talk about its nutrients. Or else do a demonstration of one of your own favorites, the same way.
- *Parents' Lunch*. Invite parents to a nutritious lunch planned and prepared by the children.
- *Nutrition for Pets*. Most nursery schools have pets. You can have a project of studying how to feed your animals nutritiously (materials are available from veterinarians, pet stores, and the United States Government Printing Office). Keep a record of what the animals are

eating, discuss what nutrients they need, and keep a record of their weights and their measurements. Point out signs by which to judge whether the animals are healthy. (Look for healthy fur or feathers, steady growth, lively behavior, usually friendly disposition, good appetite, clear eyes.) Compare these with the signs of good health in human beings.

- *Plant a Garden.* Plant some vegetables, indoors or out. Use the growth of the plants as a nutrition lesson, pointing out that they need food, water, and light to grow properly, as we do. Harvest the food, and use it as the basis for a cooking lesson. (See the index for reference to further suggestions on gardening.)
- *Food Groups Mural.* Make a mural of the Basic Four Food Groups.
- *Plants Mural.* Show some vegetables as they appear growing above and below the ground and how they look as they are marketed. Use photographs from magazines or original drawings the children have colored.
- *Food-Production Mural.* Show a dairy, an egg farm, or the raising of animals used for food.
- *Nutrition Booklets.* Have each child make an 8- or 10-page booklet of pictures about the Basic Four Food Groups to take home. Booklets might include 1 page for each food group, 1 page for fats, and 2 pages of empty-calorie foods or foods people should eat less of.
- *Drawing Foods.* Have the children draw fruits, vegetables, and other foods and talk about what they contribute to our diets. The children may want to cut their drawings out and paste them on paper plates in realistic combinations for meals.
- *Food of the Week.* Make a bulletin board featuring a food of the week. Study its nutrients, cook it, taste it, grow it, and encourage the children to tell their families about it.
- *Produce a "Movie."* Make a "movie" about the growth and development of any food (for human beings or animals) or food group. To do it, paste cut-out photographs in a long row on a roll of wrapping paper or shelf paper. Cut out a rectangular opening the size of the pictures (12″ × 12″ is a good size) in the side of a paper carton. (The box will be used open-end-up.) Make a turning mechanism by inserting two rods through holes made in the adjoin-

ing sides of the box, above and below the opening you have made for the picture. Tack the ends of the paper roll to the rods so that the pictures will show in the opening. Then roll the pictures up mostly on one rod. Have a child show the "movie" by turning the rods, and have the other children tell the story as the pictures appear.

- *Puzzles.* Make jigsaw puzzles of pictures of fruits, vegetables, or other foods, pasted to lightweight cardboard. Use them for the basis of a nutrition discussion.
- *Seasonal Foods.* Make murals or posters of foods that are characteristic of the different seasons. Discuss what we see, feel, smell, hear, at each season. Relate it to nutrition.
- *Models.* Model foods from clay or papier-mâché. Use the models to illustrate a discussion of nutrition.
- *Decorate Eggs.* At Easter or other times, decorate hard-cooked eggs (see p. 94), and use the activity as a starting point for discussing the nutritional value of eggs and egg dishes.
- *Kitchen Puppets.* Make puppets out of fresh fruits, vegetables, spoons, and kitchen utensils, or use the puppet patterns on pp. 6-7 and 10-11. Let the children discuss nutrition and good eating habits with the puppets.

Kitchen Puppets

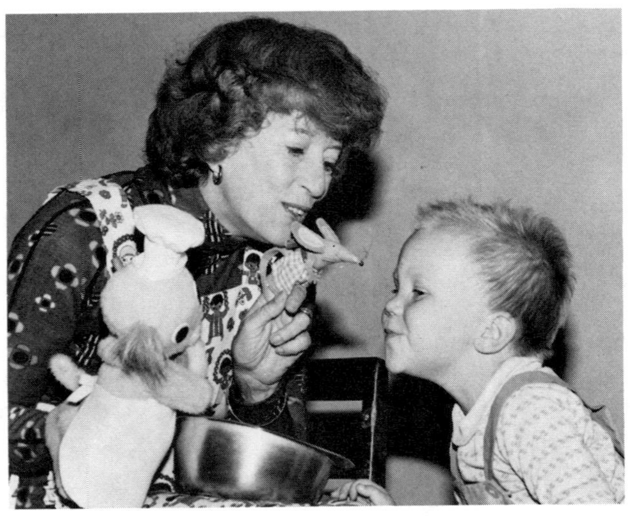

Two-year-old Joshua McClenahan seems absorbed in a discussion of cooking techniques with Mr. Hush Puppy and Ms. Parsley, as puppeteer Betsy Brown smiles.

- *Acting and Dancing.* Let the children enact the growth of plants or animals in dances or pantomimes, to the beat of drum or other music.
- *Dramatic Play.* Let the children identify themselves as their favorite foods. Use this as a basis for group selection or partner selection, for a project or activity.
- *Field Trips.* Take the children on field trips to the grocery store, a dairy, a bakery, a produce market, a restaurant, or a cafeteria, or whatever else is available that will show them another step in the "food-production chain." Be sure to make arrangements for your visit ahead of time with the management, and check with them again on the day of the trip. Particularly, take advantage of any opportunity to visit ethnic food stores. Try their special foods as a center point for a discussion of nutrition.

- *Nutrition House.* Use it to serve snacks from, to "buy" good snacks from with play "money," or to display materials related to nutrition. Make it of a large cardboard packing case, one a child can stand up in. Cut out a door, but leave the bottom half attached so a type of serving counter can be created. Decorate the box with photographs or drawings of foods, arranged by food groups. Let the older children serve or "sell" snacks or picnic lunches from the Nutrition House.
- *Nutrition Truck.* If the school has a child-size truck or a wagon, paste pictures of foods on it, and use it to deliver snacks, picnic lunches, lemonade, or juice.
- *Vitamin and Mineral Blocks.* Take 9 fairly large sturdy cartons of uniform or odd sizes (at least 12" × 12"), tape them shut, and paint them all over with water-base paints. Then paint each with the letter *A, B, C, D, K,* or *E,* or *iron, calcium,* or *phosphorous.* Brighten them even more by pasting pictures of the food sources of those vitamins and minerals on them. Use the blocks to illustrate any discussion on how vitamins and minerals help us grow and stay healthy.
- *Shoe-Box Train — The Four Food Groups Express.* Make a four-car train by punching a hole in each narrow end of four brightly decorated shoe boxes, one for each food group. Run a cord through all the holes, tying a knot inside each hole. Space the boxes as you wish. Allow enough cord at one end of the train for pulling. Cut out photographs of foods and put them in the appropriate "cars." If you use larger boxes, the children can climb in them. Introduce this as a group activity, and keep it for individual play afterward.
- Make several beanbags identified as different kinds of food, such as a glass of milk, a candy bar, a vegetable, a fruit, a hamburger, a slice of bread. Fill the most nutritious foods with the most beans, and put very few beans in the empty-calorie food bags. Then have the children try to toss the bags into a painted cutout mouth on the front of a large cardboard carton (at least 2' × 3'). Thus, the good foods will land in the mouth as they should, and the empty-calorie foods will fall short of their mark.

3

Real Cool Cooking

RECIPES THAT DON'T USE HEAT

Children can easily take part in many fundamental cooking experiences. Such activities do not all involve the application of heat. They do not even necessarily involve food. After all, children discover the fun of cooking on their own when they mix water and dirt to create their first mud pies!

Many preschool programs stress manipulative, tactile experiences with materials of such varied textures as Play-Doh, bread dough, cloud dough, sand, dirt, clay, sawdust, oatmeal, cornmeal, and finger paint. How many teachers realize that in such basic nursery-school experiences children are actually using techniques that would apply to cooking?

Children who sift sand are using the technique for sifting flour. Children who knead Play-Doh can easily knead bread dough. Children who make mud pies are learning to mix ingredients. When children are allowed to pour juice or milk (or when they playfully pour water on the floor), they are learning the control they need to master measuring. Teachers can enhance these common experiences by planning further, similar ones that stress the techniques used in cooking.

Young Children Can Cook

Children should be allowed to participate in all school cooking activities to the fullest extent possible. (Circumstances will vary according to how many children and how many teachers and teaching assistants are involved.) Two-year-olds, surprisingly, can do almost everything our cooking lessons call for, though it would be unwise to let them use knives for cutting. Most three-, four-, and five-year-olds can use knives, but under constant supervision (see p. 16).

Enrichment

Teachers can take advantage of the high degree of motivation in the cooking experiences to enrich the lessons. They can use the mathematics involved in measuring and the need to read in order to understand a recipe, to stimulate the children to learn more about arithmetic and reading. The example of the teacher's having to read and to know arithmetic can be a major impetus for children's wanting to develop those skills. In actual experiments the children can readily see the differences between measurements in their different-size containers. Point out also how the same amount of liquid reaches different levels when it is poured into variously shaped containers, and talk about the relationships between volumes. The ordinary measuring cup can be a laboratory in itself—what more practical way is there to translate written fractions into reality? Many recipes call for the recognition of geometrical shapes (triangles, squares, circles, oblongs) as well as for discerning differences in size. Teachers should stress such perceptions routinely in their cooking lessons.

Motor Skills

Cooking also offers many opportunities for the development of preschoolers' small and large muscles. The large muscles come into play in such common preparation and serving activities as wiping off tables and chairs; mopping and sweeping the floor; turning the ice-cream freezer; using an eggbeater; scraping, washing, and drying the dishes; pouring; squeezing juice; rolling dough with hands or a rolling pin; grinding a hand grinder; shaking; sifting; and stirring.

Some of the same and other activities promote small-muscle development, such as breaking, chipping ice, cracking shells, cutting and slicing, dipping, grating, grinding, leveling, measuring, mixing, peeling, pouring, pressing, rolling out, shaking, sifting, snapping, spreading, squeezing, tearing, turning, and whipping.

Starting to Cook　An obvious beginning in teaching young children to cook is to discuss various foods they encounter every day. In the discussion you can enlist their innate drive for discovery by directing their observation of those foods—their colors, smells, tastes, textures, sizes, weights, shapes, and origins (if known). A whole lesson can be designed around one piece of fruit or a vegetable. What a world of discovery there is, for example, in a single apple! A smooth, red skin—a rough, brown stem—a crisp white, juicy meat—an indescribable taste—a spherical shape—a sweet, fruity odor—seeds to plant—and the fun of changing it into applesauce!

Examining foods in their uncooked state, preparing them for serving and eating, combining them, and working with molding doughs and modeling doughs are some of the ways in which children can have real cooking experiences without using heat. There are many more. The recipes in this chapter present a range of valid experiences that can be enjoyed by children and their teachers without the use of heat sources. In addition, a similarly broad selection of stimulating recipes that do involve "hot cooking" appears in Chapter 4.

It should be noted that a few of our "cool cooking" recipes do require a bit of cooking or precooking by the teacher. And some even call for the use of a heat source during the lesson. We include them in this chapter because they involve basic cooking techniques.

Now, let's start cooking! In this chapter you'll find suggestions and recipes arranged in sections for Fruits and Vegetables (including edible flowers); Nuts and Seeds; Milk and Milk Products; Eggs; Fish, Meat, and Legumes; Spaghetti and Noodles; and Bread and Cereals (with recipes for modeling doughs). Then come Desserts and Other Sweets. Each section begins with a general lesson plan and continues with more recipes and further suggestions for enrichment activities. Recipes in each section are arranged with the simplest first and the more complex later. Remember—young children can perform all these operations with normal supervision.

COOL COOKING WITH FRUITS AND VEGETABLES

Fruits and vegetables are one of the most colorful, varied, and child-intriguing groups of foods. Nutritionally their contribution to our diet is significant—minerals, vitamins, and fiber. In working with this group we suggest teachers concentrate on expanding the children's knowledge of these foods because so many varieties are neglected in many homes. Fruits and vegetables are generally less expensive than other foods, so experiences with them are only limited by the teacher's imagination. For added fun, we include some suggestions for using garden flowers as food.

Remember always to wash any fresh fruits or vegetables before the lesson because of the common use of pesticides by growers and because of previous handling in the market.

In Class   First have the class examine the whole fruit or vegetable and discuss its size, shape, color, texture, and smell.* We have found that this is most effective when a single piece of fresh fruit

---

*(For the most part, these suggestions can also be applied to frozen, dried, or canned fruit—but only when fresh fruit is not available.)

or vegetable is the focus of a group's attention. Pass it around for each child to examine alone, and encourage each child to verbalize his or her impressions.

Then cut the fruit or vegetable in different ways. This is a good opportunity to talk about fractions and shapes. One part may be shredded, grated, diced, minced, sliced, or dipped. Another part may be peeled, to show a different way of serving. (The children can take turns doing these operations, with supervision.)

Pass enough pieces around so each child has a taste, and again encourage them to verbalize their reactions. Do not hesitate to try *all* fruits and vegetables raw, even though they commonly are prepared in other ways. A good one to try raw is the potato, which is always eaten cooked but nevertheless can be tasted raw as part of this exploration.

If a fruit or vegetable has seeds, soak them overnight for planting the next day. Carrots, beets, red and white radishes, turnips, parsnips, potatoes, sweet potatoes, or yams can be sliced off about an inch from the stem end and the stem end placed in a shallow dish with half an inch of water. If this is kept moist, the stems will develop shoots, which will continue to grow until roots develop and it can be planted.

The ideal conclusion of this lesson is to cook the fruit or vegetable by simply boiling it five or ten minutes (till easily pierced with a fork) in a small amount of water and then comparing the cooked with the raw. If there are no cooking facilities, the teacher can cook enough at home for the children to taste, and bring it in for comparison.

We have found in our classes that young children can learn to be nutrition-conscious and to know which foods provide important nutrients. With a positive approach about what *should* be eaten we have succeeded better than with a negative approach about what should not be eaten (candy, soda pop, cookies, and such). The *Good Foods Coloring Book*, which can be obtained free of charge from the United States Department of Agriculture (see p. 164 for this and other resource materials), has proved to be an excellent teaching aid for this learning.

The nutritional objective of a lesson like this should be to encourage children to eat four to five child-size servings of fruits and vegetables each day. One should be citrus fruit or tomato, one or two should be green or yellow vegetables, and the rest may be any other. Vegetables and fruits are sadly lacking in many American diets, so you might well stress the need for eating a variety of fruits and vegetables, and the value of serving them raw. We have had success with suggestions like these:

When you go to the market, ask your mother to buy some of these.
When you eat this at home, remember to tell us about it the next day.
If you have a new fruit or vegetable at home, will you bring one to share with us?
What would you like to grow in the school garden?
Let's make out tomorrow's lunch menu together.

This is an especially valuable opportunity to involve the parents in a good nutritional program for the children by sending home a reminder that children should be encouraged to eat a variety of fruits and vegetables *every day.** Remind the children that foods that cannot be purchased fresh can often be bought canned or frozen, so variety is always assured. Again, let us stress that both the parent and the teacher should be warned against unwittingly imposing their own food prejudices on impressionable children.

At other times examine a variety of fruits and vegetables, such as *different kinds* of melons, apples, oranges, bananas, squash, potatoes, grapes, pears, peaches, cherries, grape-

*We find the best time to discuss nutrition with parents first is when they are enrolling their children. At that point we explain our nutrition program fully and outline its importance to the growth and development of the children, the need to expand their food interests, and the advantages of the parents' cooperating in applying the program at home. If the subject has been discussed ahead of time with parents in this way, it is easy to send them reminders and to enlist their help from time to time as the program continues.

fruits, apricots, berries, lettuce, beans, or peas. They may be fresh, frozen, canned, or dried. (Remember, your produce man only orders what he can sell, so, if you want a variety that is not in his store, ask him to order it for you.)

Cool Recipes for Fruit

Strawberries Wash thoroughly, and drain enough for each child to have 3 or 4. Leave stems on for holding. Dip in powdered sugar, granulated sugar, orange juice or other fruit juice, whipping cream, or cinnamon and sugar mixed. Don't forget to plant some whole strawberries with their seeds in a pot, ½ inch below the surface of the soil (if you keep the soil moist, they should grow).

Fruit Salad Any number of varieties of fruit can be mixed in a salad. Just cut the larger fruits into bite-size chunks (peeled if the skin is tough or too dirty to clean), and dip the pieces into orange or lemon juice to prevent darkening. Any fruit juice makes an easy and simple dressing if you pour it on, a tablespoonful at a time, till the salad is moistened. Make enough to serve each child ¼ cup.

VARIATIONS
- For dessert, add 1 tbsp* brown sugar mixed with ½ cup sour cream or sweetened whipped cream to the fruit.
- Add marshmallows, raisins, nuts, or coconut (grated or shredded).

Bananas (or Other Fresh Fruits) Cut into bite-size pieces, and dip the pieces in fruit juice and then into coconut; cocoa; chopped nuts; white, brown, or powdered sugar; jam or jelly; peanut butter; cinnamon sugar; melted

*Abbreviations are used throughout the book for *teaspoon* (tsp) and *tablespoon* (tbsp).

chocolate, or the like. (Cinnamon sugar can be premixed by combining ½ cup sugar and 1 tsp cinnamon.)

Pureed Fruit Select very ripe fruit, and peel if skin is bitter or tough. Remove the seeds. Puree in a blender. (You may have to add a little water or fruit juice.) Sweeten to taste if necessary. Puree can be served as a pudding or a sauce. Half a cup of fruit plus 2 tbsp water yields a scant ½ cup puree.

Stuffed Fruit Slit dried dates, apricots, or plums. Fill each with a nut meat, cream cheese, peanut butter, or a marshmallow.

VARIATION

- *Sugarplums.* For an extra treat or for something special the children can take home and share, help them make sugarplums. To make 18, you need: 18 extra large tenderized prunes (about 1 pound), 18 pitted dates, 18 dried apricots, 3 tbsp peanut butter, and granulated sugar to roll them in. Place prunes in a colander or coarse strainer over boiling water, and steam, covered, 10 minutes or until plump and tender. Remove from the saucepan and cool (this can be done the day before). Make a lengthwise slit in each prune, and remove the pit. Fill each date with ½ tsp peanut butter. Enclose filled date in apricot half. Stuff each prune with a date-stuffed apricot. Push the edges of the slit together, leaving a bit of apricot showing. Roll each prune in granulated sugar, or colored sugar if you like. [To store, refrigerate in a tightly covered container (keeps several weeks). Reroll in sugar before serving.]

Fruit Shakes Use any very ripe fruit, peeling it if necessary. Blend in the blender with an equal amount of milk, adding honey or sugar (to taste), crushed ice, and vanilla or almond extract (to taste). When you use ½ cup fruit, ½ cup milk, and 2 ice cubes, the yield is 12 ounces. A child's serving is 3 or 4 ounces.

Smoothie   Peel and cut up ½ cup ripe fruit. Blend with an equal amount of any fruit juice. Add ¼ cup crushed ice, and blend again to mix thoroughly. Sweeten if necessary. Yield: 12 ounces. Some delicious combinations are: bananas, dates, and orange juice; strawberries, raspberries, and pineapple juice; pineapple, apples, and tangerine juice; and apples, pears, and apricot juice. YOU NAME IT!

Fruit Juice   Select ripe oranges, lemons, or grapefruit (1 orange or ½ lemon or ½ grapefruit per child). Cut the fruit in half, and squeeze in a hand juicer or an electric juicer. Let the children pour and serve. Orange and grapefruit juice can be drunk as is. With lemon juice, first let the children taste the plain juice and discuss *sour* and *tart*. Then add water, ice cubes, and sugar (to taste) to make lemonade. Compare these fresh juices with a variety of frozen or canned fruit juices.

Fruit Pops   Use either fresh, frozen, or canned juice or fruit puree (see p. 59), ½ cup for each child. Pour into divided ice-cube trays or 4-ounce paper cups, and insert a popsicle stick or a wooden ice-cream spoon in each portion when they are partially frozen (about 1 hour), and serve them after another hour, when they are fully frozen. This is a good way to add an extra fruit to a child's diet.

Fruit on a Stick   Cut any ripe or canned fruit into large chunks (bananas and pineapple are favorites). Use ¼ cup for each child, and allow enough extra for seconds. Spear each chunk with a toothpick or a bamboo skewer, and serve.

VARIATION

- If you wish to use heat, melt a package of chocolate chips in a double boiler with 1 tbsp cooking oil, stirring. (The oil keeps it from separating and makes it easier to spread.) Have the children dip the fruit into the melted chocolate, and put the fruit on wax paper on a paper plate, and freeze or refrigerate it until the chocolate is set.

Cool Recipes for Vegetables

Vegetable Salad Tear the leafy vegetables into small pieces, chop the soft vegetables (such as tomatoes), and grate the root vegetables. Allow ½ cup per child. Use any purchased dressing (mayonnaise, sour cream, French dressing, and cole-slaw dressing are all favorites with children).

Carrot and Raisin Salad Shred 2 cups peeled carrots into a bowl. Toss with ½ cup raisins. Stir in ¼ cup to ½ cup mayonnaise. Yield: 8 child-size servings.

Cole Slaw Shred 2 cups cabbage. Toss with ¼ cup to ½ cup mayonnaise or other dressing. Yield: 8 child-size servings.

VARIATIONS

- Add ¼ cup crushed pineapple.
- Use 1½ cups green cabbage with ½ cup red cabbage.
- Add ¼ cup shredded carrots.
- Add ¼ cup each chopped nuts, raisins, and baby marshmallows.
- Add ¼ cup chopped celery.
- Add ¼ tsp toasted sesame seeds, celery seeds, or caraway seeds.

Vegetable Juice Make vegetable juice in a blender by adding cut-up vegetables and water. Allow ½ cup vegetables and ¼ cup water. Salt to taste. Suggestions: celery, carrots, beets, tomatoes, cucumbers, zucchini.

Green Snacks Stuff celery or cucumbers (split the long way and hollowed out with a spoon) with cheese (cream, cottage, grated cheddar, or cheese spread). Each child would want half a stalk of celery or half a cucumber with 1 tbsp cheese.

Fingers Were Made Before Forks   Peel and cut up in small pieces, carrots, celery, radishes, zucchini, cauliflower, cucumbers, jicama, and the like to serve as finger-food snacks or with lunch. Cover closely with plastic wrap, and refrigerate until serving. Allow 2 to 3 choices per child.

Tomato Flowers   Cut fresh tomatoes in fourths, sixths, or eighths, making sure not to cut them completely apart at the bottoms. Spread the wedges apart at the tops so they look like the petals of a flower. Fill the centers with cottage cheese, tuna-fish salad, egg salad, or the like. Top each with a crosswise slice of hard-cooked egg for the center of the flower. Allow 1 small tomato and ¼ cup filling per child.

Pretty Peas   For 8 children buy about 1 pound of fresh peas. Shell them, and eat some raw, plant some, and cook the rest for lunch.

To cook peas, place them in a saucepan, cover them with water, and bring to a boil. Cover, and cook until tender (about 5 minutes). Drain, and add salt and butter.

To plant peas, make holes in the soil about 1 inch deep and about 4 inches apart. Drop 1 pea in each, cover them, and keep the soil moist. (Peas grow very quickly.) Peas can also be grown on wet cotton or blotting paper placed inside a glass jar. Keep moist, and the peas will sprout in a few days.

Unpopped Corn   Let the children husk corn and taste it raw. (For 8 children, allow 4 ears of corn for cooking and 1 ear for tasting and planting.) Cook the remaining ears for lunch by dropping them into boiling water 5 to 8 minutes. Overcooking makes corn tough. Plant some of the kernels, following the directions for planting peas (above).

Lettuce or Spinach Fingers   Spread clean lettuce or spinach leaves, 1 per child, with softened cream cheese or with cottage cheese. Roll them up, and place them on a plate, seam side down. Chill, and serve for a snack.

Edible Flowers   Children are surprised to learn that they can eat some of the flowers they see in their gardens. But you must caution them *strongly* against eating anything that might be poisonous, so *be* *careful* not to introduce this to children younger than four years old. We eat many parts of different plants—tubers, roots, leaves, flowers, or stems—and, while some parts of a plant may be edible, other parts of that same plant may be poisonous. For example, the leaves of the rhubarb are poisonous, even though we eat the stems. Since the list of plants they can't eat is endless, you might suggest that the children eat only those parts that you or their mothers serve them. They can eat the following, for example, though they may find some parts bitter.

artichoke	cauliflower	mustard	rose petals
broccoli	geraniums	nasturtiums	squash blossoms

Flowers have the same general nutritional value as other vegetables. This is mainly for a tasting experience, but squash blossoms can be fried in butter, nasturtiums can be used in salad, and rose petals are sometimes used in jams and preserves.

Poisonous Plant *Poisonous Parts*

autumn crocus *bulbs*
azalea *leaves, flowers*
belladonna *berries*
black locust *young leaves, bark, seeds*
bleeding heart *leaves, tubers*
buckeye, or horse chestnut *leaves, fruits*
*castor bean *seeds (beans)*
cherry *stone, wilted leaves*

Poisonous Plant *Poisonous Parts*

*daffodil *bulbs*
*daphne *bark, leaves, fruits*
*delphinium *young plants, seeds*
English ivy *leaves, berries*
*foxglove *leaves, flowers*
garden amaryllis (naked lady) *bulbs*
holly *berries*
horse chestnut, or buckeye *leaves, fruits*

continued

*Very poisonous.
(This is not a complete list, so check your library for information on plants that are native to your area.)

Poisonous Plant *Poisonous Parts*

hydrangea *leaves, buds*
*lantana *leaves, green berries*
*larkspur *young plants, seeds*
*lily of the valley *leaves, flowers, roots*
lupine *all parts*
milkweed *leaves, stems*
monkshood *all parts*
mountain laurel *leaves, twigs, flowers*
*narcissus *bulbs*
*oleander *all parts, including smoke from
burning*

Poisonous Plant *Poisonous Parts*

opium poppy *juice of unripe capsules*
peach *seeds, wilted leaves*
philodendron *stems, leaves*
plum *seeds, wilted leaves*
privet *berries*
rhododendron *leaves, flowers*
wisteria *seeds*
wonderberry (garden huckleberry) *unripe
berries, leaves*
yellow jessamine (*also* yellow jasmine) *all parts*
yew *all parts*

Planting Vegetables Children love to start their own gardens at school, either in a small plot or indoors in containers. Plan on growing some plants that grow above the ground and some that grow below. The list, of course, is virtually endless, but these are some that have been most successful with us: (1) above ground: apple tree, cauliflower, corn, lettuce, orange tree, pea, pumpkin, squash, string bean, tomato, watermelon; (2) below ground: carrot, onion, parsnip, potato, radish (this grows very fast).

If #10 (gallon-size) cans are available, they can be used as planters (one for each child or plant) by puncturing two or three drainage holes in the bottoms with a beer-can opener. Use soil from the yard or planting soil, mixing ⅛ part peat moss with either. The children can take their plants home without transplanting when the plants are 2 or 3 inches high.

If we are planting small plants or a single plant, we usually plant them in containers small enough to take home. For this we use paper cups or cottage-cheese containers or peat pots

---

*Very poisonous.

(made of pressed peat and shaped into small pots) purchased from a nursery or plant center. The advantage of peat pots is that they can be placed directly into the ground when the children take them home. We would use the #10 cans if we were starting several plants at the same time. The children are impatient to take the plants home, so when the plants are tall enough to have a few leaves, we let them.

One of the best planting experiences we ever had was with starting a lima bean in a small plastic bag with 2 tbsp soil and ½ tsp water. When you do this, you close the top of the bag and pin it up on a bulletin board or any surface near the sunlight. When the bean starts to grow, the children can see the development on top and below the surface. It does not have to be watered, as the moisture stays in the bag. Replant when the sprout is ready to grow out of the bag, although you may leave it there if you make a small hole in the bag for the sprout to grow through.

Food on a Stick To make familiar foods attractive and to illustrate a different way of cooking and serving, combine various fruits, vegetables, meat, and cheeses and thread several together on round lollipop sticks or skewers, to be eaten raw or cooked. This is an exciting way for children to eat vegetables and fruits for salads, desserts, and snacks. Use about 1-inch cubes, as larger pieces are difficult to handle, and smaller pieces fall apart when pierced. Don't forget to serve them for snacks, especially when the children have made them. Do not hesitate to combine fruits and vegetables. Let the children suggest combinations they want to try.

VARIATIONS

- *Fresh Fruit on a Stick*. Cut pieces of fresh apples, pears, melons, peaches, apricots, bananas. Combine with canned or thawed frozen fruits. Dip each piece of fresh fruit in pineapple, orange, or lemon juice to keep it from darkening. Thread on sticks in any order the children wish. (The fruit can be brushed with melted jam or jelly, for variety.)
- *Vegetables on a Stick*. Radishes, cherry tomatoes, carrots, cucumbers, pickles, olives,

cauliflower, string beans, green peppers, beets, cooked potatoes, lima beans, and thawed frozen vegetables make a colorful combination.
- Cheeses, sausages, and lunch meats may be combined with fruit or vegetable combinations or used alone.
- Any of the above combinations may be brushed with a sauce to prevent excessive drying, put on a baking sheet, and baked at 350° for 10 minutes. Suggestions for sauces are: fruit juice, beef broth, melted jam or jelly, soy sauce, tomato sauce, catsup, or chili sauce.
- Interesting variations are such ground meats as beef, lamb, veal, and meat-loaf mixture made into 1-inch meatballs. Alternate them with pieces of lunch meat, salami, or sausage. Or alternate meat with fruit or vegetables. Bake as directed above. Imagination and creativity are the only limitations to the combinations and fun the children can have with this recipe.

ENRICHMENTS

- Children can learn the word *kabob,* since it is so commonly used for this kind of food.
- Since these are so easy to prepare, the children can make an assortment of kabobs for a party for parents or for other children. They can be made in advance, covered, and refrigerated until time to serve.
- If possible, borrow a table hibachi, or else make one by using a large metal pail with a grate of some kind over the top. Put a few pieces of charcoal in the hibachi, ignite them, let them burn down to glowing embers, and cook the kabobs over the coals much as prehistoric people did. This gives rise to interesting discussions of how people lived in times gone by, before we had the conveniences of the technological age. It goes without saying that safety precautions are necessary. Put the hibachi on a metal cookie sheet before setting it on the table. Handle the skewers with tongs until they are cool enough to handle with bare hands. Be sure the room is *well* ventilated. This also might be fun to do outside.

COOL COOKING WITH NUTS AND SEEDS

Nuts are high in fat and calories, and yet they are a good source of vegetable protein.

In Class Buy several varieties of nuts in their shells, shelled, and in cans (dry-roasted and salted). Let the children crack them, if necessary, and taste them. Talk about the differences in flavor, color, shape, size, and texture. You can find most of the following nuts and seeds in markets:

acorn	cardamom	coriander	pecan	pumpkin
allspice	carob	filbert	peppercorn	sesame
almond	cashew	macadamia	pine	sunflower
Brazil	chestnut	nutmeg (whole)	pistachio	vanilla bean (whole)
caraway	clove	peanut	poppy	walnut

Put those that are not already toasted into a 350° oven in a flat pan or pie plate about 10 minutes, or until golden brown. If you have coconut, grate it before toasting.

Try planting raw nuts in their shells in pots to take home or outdoors to grow at school. Give them sunlight, and keep them moist.

Coconut Colors Coconut can be tinted by placing the grated or shredded meat in a jar and adding food coloring. Shake until thoroughly impregnated. Tinted green, it makes good "grass" to hold small candy Easter eggs on top of lightly frosted cupcakes.

Peanut Butter Make your own peanut butter (or any other nut butter) by the following method: Place 1 cup shelled nuts in the jar of your blender. Add 1 or 2 tbsp bland salad oil. Blend at medium speed until desired consistency is reached—smooth, crunchy, or in-between. It may be necessary to stop and remove the massed peanuts from around the blender's blades with a rubber spatula once or twice. Add 1 or 2 tbsp sugar or honey, and ¼ tsp salt if nuts are unsalted. Blend again to mix. Yield: 1 cup.

COOL COOKING WITH MILK, CHEESE, AND OTHER MILK PRODUCTS

Milk and milk products are one of the Basic Four Food Groups. Milk is our best source of calcium and riboflavin, and it is an excellent complete protein. It is one of the best nutritional packages available, in whatever form it is consumed.

All children are familiar with milk, since it is their first food. Children are so accustomed to fluid milk that the best starting point may be to make them aware of the variety of foods that are made with milk. Some children who do not like fluid milk will accept it in such other forms.

In Class Reconstitute milk from powdered or dry skim milk, and explain to the children that you are adding the water that has been removed. (Follow the directions on the package.)

Color milk with several food colorings. Have the children talk about their reactions. Some will find they do not like milk in some colors.

Give each child a small tasting cup, and serve a variety of milks such as buttermilk, condensed milk, evaporated milk, milk shakes, and chocolate milk. Taste, and compare.

If you wish, you can simmer an unopened can of sweetened condensed milk in water (to cover) three hours until it caramelizes. You will then have *dulce de leche,* a sweet milk dessert popular in Latin America. Chill before opening the can on both ends and sliding it out as a pudding. Let the children taste plain sweetened condensed milk for comparison.

Buy a variety of cheeses, and let the children sample them. The average American has not explored the many kinds that are available. Try the foreign-food markets for unusual varieties.

Make cheese balls by creaming soft cream cheese until it is fluffy and then rolling acorn-sized amounts between the palms of the hands. Dip into chopped nuts or shredded coconut. Chill until firm, and eat plain as snacks.

Make yogurt by heating a quart of reconstituted skim milk to 98.6° (comfortable when tested on the inside of your wrist). Add to ¼ cup commercial yogurt in an earthenware or plastic container, and mix well. Cover and put in a warm place until the next day. (The pilot light in a gas oven keeps the oven at the right temperature.) Notice how it thickens. After it has thickened fully, chill. Mix with fruit, add flavoring, or eat as a topping. Reserve ¼ cup of the plain yogurt to start more yogurt with, if you wish.

Half a cup of yogurt cheese can be made by wrapping 1 cup of the homemade yogurt in a large piece of cheesecloth, tying opposite corners together (making a "hobo bundle"), and hanging it on a faucet over a sink to drip overnight. Remove from cheesecloth, and chill. This will taste like cream cheese with a tart flavor. Eat it plain, over fruit, or spread on bread or crackers.

Curds and Whey   Since most nursery-school children know "Little Miss Muffet," they enjoy making curds and whey. The curds are what we know as cottage cheese before it is separated from the liquid whey. Cottage cheese can be made from milk coagulated by rennin or rennet (junket, as it is known commercially): Heat a quart of fresh skim milk to 98.6°. Stir in two crushed rennin tablets that have been dissolved in 2 tsp cold water. Let stand until fully gelled. Cut the curd into coarse (half-inch) pieces. Reheat in a double boiler to 98.6°, and hold at that temperature until the whey separates from the curd. Drain in a cheesecloth bag over a bowl until dripping stops. Break up the curd, and mix in ½ tsp salt and 2 tbsp cream.

Ice-Milk Shake Crush 8 ice cubes, by putting them in a double plastic bag, and having the children take turns pounding it with a hammer or mallet. Put the ice in a blender with ⅔ cup water, ⅔ cup powdered milk, 2 tbsp sugar or honey (or to taste), 1 tsp vanilla or other flavoring extract, and an egg (if desired). Blend until frothy. Yield: about 16 ounces.

Artificial sweetener may be used to cut the calorie content, but this should be done only with the advice of a doctor. Since there is controversy about the use of artificial sweeteners, it is generally accepted that it should be kept at a minimum, especially for children, since a child's tolerance is less than an adult's.

Peanut-Butter Milk Shake Put 2 cups cold nonfat or regular milk into a blender. Add ⅓ cup peanut butter, commercial or homemade (see above). Add 2 tbsp sugar or honey. Crush and add 6 to 8 ice cubes. Blend until smooth. Yield: 24 ounces.

Milksicles Combine 2 cups whole milk, ½ cup instant dry milk powder, ½ cup sugar, 2 drops food coloring, and 1 tsp flavoring (vanilla, banana, or strawberry), or ¼ tsp almond or mint extract in a bowl, and stir well to blend. Pour into paper cups or into a divided ice-cube tray. Freeze about an hour. Insert a plastic spoon in each helping. Return to refrigerator, and freeze completely (about 2 hours). Allow to set at room temperature about 5 minutes before serving. Paper cups should peel off easily. Yield: six 4-ounce pops or twelve 2-ounce pops (ice-cube size).

Ice-Cream Sodas Put 1 tbsp ice-cream in the bottom of a tall glass. Add 1 tbsp any flavor syrup. Mix, and add carbonated water to fill the glass halfway. Add a scoop of ice-cream, and fill with carbonated water. Serve with a straw. This can also be made with any flavor of soda water and ice-cream, omitting the syrup. One quart of soda makes 8 child-size drinks.

VARIATIONS

- You can make the famous New York egg cream by mixing 2 tbsp chocolate syrup and 2 tbsp milk thoroughly in a 6-ounce glass and adding soda water to fill, stirring constantly. It will foam and make a satisfying mess.
- Substitute sherbet for the ice-cream to make a freeze.

Instant Puddings Use any packaged instant pudding, and follow the directions on the box. Serve in individual paper cups. One package yields 8 child-size servings.

VARIATIONS

- With vanilla pudding the children can add flavorings or coloring.
- Combine the pudding with nuts, raisins, marshmallows, cherries, fruit, chocolate chips, or coconut.
- Layer two or three different flavors or colors of pudding for contrast. As you mix the second layer, the first layer thickens in the dish, and so on.
- One of the most interesting projects we have done at our school is to use instant chocolate pudding for finger painting. Make it ahead of time, and do not tell the children it is edible. What an exciting thrill when they discover their old friend chocolate pudding in a new disguise! Each child should have about ¼ cup to work with.

Butter Divide 1 pint heavy whipping cream (preferably aged about two days in the refrigerator) evenly among 6 or so clean baby-food jars (1 for each child). Cover securely with lids (screw-on lids preferred). Take time to check. Have children shake jars until butter forms (about 5 minutes). Children may count during this period or sing a song or possibly do rhythms in their places. Let them chant, "shake, shake, shake," if they like. Open jars, and drain buttermilk into paper cups. Encourage the children to taste it. It is delicious and not like the store kind! Yield: ½ pound butter.

This is sweet butter. That is, butter without salt. Some of the butter could be salted lightly and tasted, to show the contrast in the flavors. Spread butter on crackers or bread, using butter spreaders or table knives. The children may eat some of the butter they have made themselves, and you might suggest taking home what remains in their own jars. On hot days, the butter will be very soft. Refrigerate.

VARIATIONS

- Make butter with a rotary eggbeater, an electric beater, or a blender.
- Taste margarine, and compare. Discuss the facts that margarine is made from vegetable oil and butter is made from animal fat. The vegetable oil is polyunsaturated, so it is lower in cholesterol.
- Melt butter over a *low* flame. Paint it on crackers with a pastry brush. Discuss the differences in consistency and the difference in the way melted and unmelted butter are handled, and point out that the change is caused by the application of heat.

ENRICHMENTS

- Use this experience as a starting point for a discussion of farms, dairies, cows, milk, milking, bottling, and cheeses. Use pictures from books, magazines, or other sources to illustrate.
- Point out the change in color from the off-white cream to the yellow butter.
- Point out the texture change. Use adjectives that specifically describe the textures, such as *soft, liquid, fluffy, plastic, watery*.
- Tie in this experiment with a trip to a dairy or to a market to inspect the milk and dairy cases.
- Discuss the care and storage of milk and milk products (refrigeration is necessary to keep

milk from souring and spoiling). Leave some milk out of the refrigerator, and watch it sour as the bacteria grow, and then mold. If you have a microscope, use it here.
- Visit a milk bottling plant.

Milk Cubes Soften 1 tbsp unflavored gelatin in ¼ cup cold water 5 minutes in a large bowl. Add ¾ cup boiling water, and mix thoroughly. Add 1 cup reconstituted skim milk or ⅓ cup powdered milk dissolved in 1 cup fluid whole milk, ⅓ cup sugar, and 1 tsp almond extract or 1 tsp vanilla extract. Pour into an 8″ × 8″ baking pan. Refrigerate until firm. Cut in 1-inch cubes. Servings may be topped with 2 cups fresh, frozen, or canned fruit. This is an excellent way to include milk in the diet. Yield: sixty-four 1-inch cubes.

VARIATIONS
- Vary the flavoring by using 1 tsp vanilla or banana extract, or ½ tsp mint or anise extract.
- Use such fruit-flavored gelatins as apple, banana, cherry, strawberry, and raspberry (the sour ones may curdle the milk a little, but this is harmless), and omit the sugar and extract. The proportions should be 1 package flavored gelatin to 1 cup boiling water and 1 cup milk. Prepare as directed above.
- The recipe can also be made with chocolate milk.
- Add 2 more tbsp gelatin in Step 1. This makes a very firm gelatin that can be eaten by hand (an excellent snack).
- Combine the milk cubes with fruit gelatin in the same dish. The contrasts of color and flavor are interesting and tasty.
- Instead of water, add the same amount of fruit juice.
- Pour into an ice-cube tray, and use the divider to form sections.
- This can be frozen for an interesting texture. Insert a toothpick in each section after an hour to make milk pops. Chocolate-milk gelatin (above) can also be frozen.

COOL COOKING WITH EGGS

Because eggs are fragile, children have limited experience with them. This is unfortunate because eggs intrigue children, and they are comparatively inexpensive. Lessons with eggs are good at any time, but they are especially apt in spring and around Easter.

Eggs are one of the best nutrition packages known. There are only 75 calories in a large egg, and it contains complete proteins,* iron, and small amounts of Vitamin A and Vitamin B. Children should be encouraged to eat an egg a day, or at least three or four a week. Even though eggs are considered to have high cholesterol content, there is still insufficient evidence for eliminating them from the diet—especially from children's diets. If children dislike eggs, it may be because of the way eggs are prepared for them. In this case, eggs might be served in eggnog, custard, or puddings. Eggs are one food that can be eaten at any meal. And they can be prepared in so many ways that it is unfortunate people have relegated them largely to breakfast.

In Class • Post pictures of birds and eggs on the bulletin board.
• Try to find a bird's nest to show the children. If it isn't in use, bring it to class.

---

*Proteins with all essential amino acids.

- Incubate fertile eggs purchased from a local farm or hatchery. You can buy a small incubator from a toy store or a pet store, with all directions for operating it (directions must be followed carefully). This is a thrilling experiment for children who have never seen it. Be sure to time it so chicks are born on a school day. (The process takes about 21 days.) And be prepared to keep chicks warm after birth.
- Bring in a variety of eggs (duck, chicken, pigeon, and such) if you can, or else get brown and white eggs in various sizes. Break them open, and examine them. Separate the whites from the yolks, being careful not to get any yolk in with the whites (for directions, see p. 97). If you do, you can use a piece of broken eggshell to dip it out. Whip the whites (see recipe for meringues, p. 155).
- Prepare hard-cooked eggs (p. 94). Crack and peel. Save the shells, and color them with food coloring for mosaics and other art projects.
- Color eggs at various times during the year. Don't save them just for Easter. Make Halloween eggs, Thanksgiving eggs, and so on. Let the children use their imaginations. Use food coloring in warm water (with a small amount of vinegar to set the color).
- Make stuffed eggs (recipe, p. 95).
- Blow uncooked eggs by puncturing both ends of the shell with a sharp needle. Enlarge one hole to ¼ inch, and blow the contents out that hole into a bowl. Demonstrate, and then have each child try it on his or her own egg. Caution them not to hold the eggs so tightly they break. Save the contents for scrambled eggs or custard (pp. 96 and 95). Decorate the shells by painting or dyeing, or by pasting trimmings on them. Remember to recite "Humpty Dumpty."
- It can be fun for the class to keep an "egg-eating chart" for a week. Have the children draw or post a representation of an egg after their names whenever they eat one at home or at school.

COOL COOKING WITH FISH, MEAT, AND LEGUMES

This group of foods is an outstanding source of animal protein, iron, and B vitamins. Dried peas and beans (legumes) and nuts are included because their nutritional contribution is similar.

In Class   Animals, birds, and fish are extremely interesting and appealing to children—especially to city children. It is very important to talk with them about the difference between raising animals for food and having them at home as pets.

The class may want to raise a pet as a group project, or they may accumulate a file of pictures of animals that are raised for food around the world.

You can plan field trips to the zoo, to a farm, to a packing house, to a dairy, to a poultry ranch, or to a pet shop. Always be sure to make arrangements with the hosts for your visit and to check again that morning or the day before, to remind them that you are coming. Also remember to check the school medical charts to see whether any of the children have allergies that might be a problem.

Meat charts from the California Beef Council or similar organizations showing how animals are sectioned for different cuts of meat (see p. 163) can be interesting to children.

And they will enjoy the transformation if you turn a bouillon cube into soup for them.

Cool Cooking with Fish and Meat

Sashimi (raw fish) is eaten by the Japanese, and the more enterprising teacher might want to buy a variety of *very fresh*, raw fish, slice it very thin, and serve it on crackers. Possibilities are such mild fish as halibut, red snapper, salmon, sea bass, and sole.

A tasting session with canned fish, such as tuna, salmon, sardines, and jack mackerel, and with fresh, canned, or frozen shellfish, such as shrimp, crabs, oysters, clams, lobsters, scallops, mussels, abalone, and crayfish, could be a dramatic accompaniment to a science lesson on fish and shellfish.

Buy a whole fish to make a fish print with or to dissect. Be *sure* the fish is fresh, and use it as soon as possible. If thawed, use immediately. And remember that the common negative adult attitude about fish can also be communicated to children.

Dissecting a Fish When you buy a fish to dissect, have the market leave the guts in. Slit the fish down the front, and point out the similarities between fish organs and human organs. Also examine the bone structure and the gills. Get as involved as the children want to be.

Fish Prints Spread a small amount of black block-printing ink over one side of a whole fresh fish with a brayer or a small paint roller. Press a sheet of rice paper or newsprint against the fish, being careful to press the entire side of the fish against the paper, especially the head and tail. Remove the sheet of paper, and allow it to dry thoroughly. Each child in the class can make a print from the same fish, applying more ink as needed.

Grinding Meat Children enjoy grinding meat in a hand grinder. Except for pork, any fresh ground meat can safely be tasted raw.

Sausage An assortment of smoked sausage might be purchased for the children to test in small pieces. If the sausages are not smoked, you can cook them at home and bring them to school. If you are lucky enough to have a sausage factory near your school, plan a trip so the children can see how they are made.

Beef Jerky Buy jerky in individual pieces. Tell how the pioneers and explorers used to carry beef jerky with them because it would not spoil, took little space, and provided energy food.

Tuna Salad Mix 1 can of tuna (drained), ½ cup chopped celery, and ¼ cup mayonnaise. Chill and serve.

Cool Cooking with Legumes (or Pulses)

Buy a variety of dried peas, lentils, and other beans from the grocery. (There is tremendous variety in the colors and shapes of green peas, black-eyed peas, split peas (yellow and green), red beans, lima beans (white and green), kidney beans, white beans, black beans, pinto beans, northern beans, and the rest.) Compare their colors, textures, and sizes.

Planting Beans   Soak at least one bean per child overnight, and put them into an open glass jar or drinking glass, beans on the outside with damp cotton or a damp blotter in the center. Put the container in the light so the children can watch the sprouts. In a few days the beans will start to sprout. The sprouts can be planted when they are about two inches high, or they can be eaten as sprouts in 3 or 4 days.

Layered Legumes   Layer the dried beans or peas in a mason jar for contrast of color and shape. This makes a beautiful gift for the children to take home to their mothers, if the beans are packed tightly enough so they do not move out of the layers.

Legume Collages   Have the class make collages by gluing peas and beans on paper plates or on cardboard.

Beans and More Beans   Compare the tastes of canned kidney beans, refried beans, and baked beans with dried legumes.

COOL COOKING WITH SPAGHETTI AND NOODLES (PASTA)

Since all pasta is basically of one of two types (either noodles with egg, or spaghetti and macaroni without egg), serve the children your usual spaghetti sauce (or a canned one) over different shapes of both kinds (see recipe, p. 104).

Most grocery stores carry a variety of spaghetti and noodles, but if you know of an Italian grocery store, you can find a wealth of shapes and sizes of pasta there to use in many art projects.

Pasta Collage Collect cigar or other boxes, and have the children decorate the tops with various shapes of pasta. Fasten them in place with white glue. When the glue is dry, paint them with brushes or spray paint.

Christmas Wreaths An easy-to-assemble Christmas project can be to decorate 45 rpm records with pasta on one side and spray them gold. Finish the tops of the "wreaths" with colorful bows. Run a 10-inch thread through the center hole, and tie it in a bow at the edge of the record to make a hanging arrangement.

COOL COOKING WITH BREAD AND CEREALS

Bread, cereal grain, and products made from them make up one of the Basic Four Food Groups. Their nutritional contribution—calories, iron, and Vitamin B—is substantial because these foods are eaten often. Children should have ample opportunity for experience with them. We would like to emphasize the importance both of eating whole-grain products and of variety. The loaf of white bread—so popular—is the least nutritious of all bread products. The teacher can help children expand their horizons by offering them varieties of breads and cereals they may not see at home.

Molding and Modeling Materials

A good starting place for bread activities could be making and working with the molding and modeling materials, since this involves techniques similar to those used in making real bread.

Whenever possible, allow the children to mix the dough, because this is half the fun. If they work at one table, they will enjoy the socializing, and clean-up will be easier.

Add any food coloring with the liquid, so it is dispersed evenly throughout the dough. We also add a few drops of oil of clove, oil of wintergreen, oil of peppermint, or any other flavoring to any of these except the Peanut Butter Fudge Dough, because they add a pleasant aroma while the children are working with dough and they keep the dough from getting rancid. This also gives you an opportunity to add words such as *pound, roll, flatten,* and *firm* to the children's vocabularies and to talk about the smells with them. Each of these recipes will yield enough for a class of around 12 children. The simplest recipes appear first.

Clay Dough

6 cups flour   6 cups salt   6 tbsp powdered alum (available at drugstores)   water
Mix dry ingredients. Add water slowly while mixing well with a spoon. Continue mixing with hands until dough feels like clay. Figures made of this will harden in the air. To keep, shape the dough into balls, wrap each ball in a damp cloth, and store in a covered container.

Baker's Clay

2 cups flour   1 cup salt   1 tbsp oil   ¾ cup water (approximately)   food coloring (optional)
Mix to the consistency of bread dough. Store in a covered container, or it will dry out.

Cloud Dough

6 cups flour   1 cup salad oil   water   food coloring (optional)
Add enough water to make dough soft and pliable. This dough is soft and elastic and does not harden. Keep it in covered containers or in a plastic bag.

Cornstarch-Soda Clay

1 cup cornstarch   2 cups baking soda   1¼ cups water   food coloring
Mix in a saucepan until thoroughly blended. Cook over medium heat about 4 minutes, stirring constantly until mixture thickens to consistency of moist mashed potatoes. Cover with damp cloth to cool. Knead as you would dough. Keep covered with a damp cloth when not in use, as it dries hard if not kept moist. Figures made with this dough can be painted after they

harden and then sprayed with clear plastic or coated over with white glue thinned with an equal amount of water after the paint is thoroughly dry.

Cooked Molding Dough

2 cups salt   1 cup cornstarch   1⅓ cups water
Combine salt and ⅔ cup water. Bring to a boil. Mix cornstarch with ⅔ cup water, and stir until smooth. Combine the two mixtures. This dough is smooth, pliable, spongy, and snowy white if no coloring is added. Keep in a plastic bag, or it will dry out.

Peanut Butter Fudge Dough

1 cup peanut butter (any style)   1¼ cups non-fat powdered milk   6-8 tbsp pureed fruit (Baby fruit works very well; canned or cooked fruit may be pureed in the blender. Do not include any of the liquid.)

Cream peanut butter; gradually mix in powdered milk. Add pureed fruit, a tablespoon at a time, until desired consistency is reached. Form into balls. Give each child a ball for molding and eating. Decorate with chocolate chips, chocolate sprinkles, coconut, or any other edible decoration, or roll in granola, wheat germ, or crushed dry cereal. Cover to keep moist.

Gunk

Courtesy of Norma Lowry
2 pounds cornstarch   3¾ cups water   food coloring
Add a few drops of food coloring to the water, and stir it into the cornstarch. When the cornstarch is dissolved, drop the whole batch onto a table top for the children to play with. Gunk is almost liquid, which makes an interesting change from other doughs and clays. This is the cleanest of the messy activities because, when the gunk dries, it can be swept away. Any that is left over can be stored in a clean jar and allowed to dry out. It can be reconstituted by adding water.

Bread

Bread Dough

Make a dough from the pretzel recipe on page 117, and let the children practice rolling, cutting, braiding, twisting, and kneading it. Or roll the dough out, and let them cut it into shapes.

These do not need to be baked. Allow them to air dry until firm. These are for decorative use only.

Sandwich Filling Station Let the children make their own sandwiches at the table with a variety of purchased breads and fillings. For example, they can spread the bread with butter, margarine, or mayonnaise and any of the following: peanut butter, cream cheese, cottage cheese, ham salad, tuna salad, egg salad, sardines, salami, cheese spreads, or slices of cheese.

Bakery Shop As a tasting experience, buy a variety of breads and let the children sample some of each. Discuss the color, appearance, flavor, and grain in each. (Try French, Italian, sourdough, pumpernickel, rye, sweet, oatmeal, whole-wheat, and corn bread, as well as variety rolls and muffins, for example.) What is not eaten can be frozen for later use.

Cracker Shop Or buy and serve crackers of various flavors and shapes. Many come in geometric shapes the children may recognize. Use the crackers as bases for sandwich spreads after you have sampled and discussed them.

Easter At Easter buy (or make) hot cross buns.

Passover At Passover, buy matzo wafers, the traditional unleavened bread eaten at that holiday. Tell the children that when the Hebrews had to flee Egypt suddenly, there was not enough time to allow the bread to rise, as usual, and people eat this bread nowadays to remind themselves of that special time long ago.

Tortillas Introduce tortillas, which may be purchased or made, if masa harina (ground corn flour) is available (there is a recipe for tortillas on the package). Spread warm tortillas thinly with butter, and taste. Compare the taste, texture, odor, shape, and color with other breads. Explain that tortillas are eaten mostly in Latin America.

Arabic Bread   Pita, a round flat bread also known as Arabic bread, is interesting if available. It is often torn and the center stuffed with sandwich filling.

Chinese Treats   Chinese dim sum (tea dumplings with savory fillings) can be a new experience for many children if there is a Chinese store or restaurant nearby where you can buy them.

Our Own Bread   Let the children make an "experimental bread" by adding honey, herbs, variety flour, spices, or the like to a basic bread recipe (as on p. 112).

COOL COOKING WITH DESSERTS AND OTHER SWEETS

Although desserts are not made of a single food group, they are nevertheless a very important and distinct part of our cultural eating pattern. It is very difficult to define a policy on serving these foods in a nursery school curriculum because of their value in children's minds. Many desserts contain sugar, which in excess can cause tooth decay and loss of appetite for more nutritious foods. The habit of eating too much sugar can later lead to the development of diabetes or hypoglycemia. Desserts are nutritionally the least desirable foods, so we suggest serving them sparingly. We include them here because they are an excellent starting point from which to develop children's interest in cooking, because cooking favorite foods opens the door into the total area of cooking. It should be stressed to the children that eating too many sweets is a particularly troublesome nutritional problem. Teachers should also bear this in mind when planning their cooking curriculums.

Baked Coconut Puncture the eyes of a coconut with an ice pick (the teacher should do this), and drain the coconut water (sometimes incorrectly called coconut milk) into a container for tasting. Bake the coconut in a pan ½ hour at 350°. When it is cool enough to handle, hit it with a hammer to crack its shell, and then peel the shell off. Cut the coconut meat in sections, and grate it, or put it into a blender with some of the coconut water or fresh milk. If there is no oven at school, do the baking at home.

Painted Cookies and Marshmallows Paint prebaked or packaged cookies (sugar cookies and animal crackers work best) or marshmallows, with food coloring slightly diluted with water using small brushes.

Sprinkled Cookies Paint cookies with simple syrup or bottled corn syrup, and then sprinkle with colored sugar while the syrup is still moist, or else frost the cookies with tinted frosting (recipe, p. 86). Simple syrup is made with 1 cup sugar and 1 cup water, just brought to a boil to dissolve the sugar, and then cooled.

Cookie Stacks Put any number of cookies together with frosting (recipe, p. 86) between layers.

Pudding Mix instant pudding according to the directions on the package, and use it for finger painting (see p. 71). Open a variety of canned puddings to taste and compare.

Popcorn Strings Make or buy popcorn, and let each child string some to use on a Christmas tree or as a necklace. Use heavy cotton thread, doubled, and #1 tapestry needles. The colored unpopped kernels make a beautiful collage, too.

Easy Cool Cookies Coat a 9″ × 13″ baking pan with ½ cup melted butter or margarine. Layer ingredients in the pan in this order (from the bottom up): ½ cup graham-cracker crumbs, 1 cup shredded coconut, 6 ounces semisweet chocolate bits, 3 ounces butterscotch bits. Pour 15 ounces sweetened condensed milk over all. Top with 1 cup chopped walnuts. Chill thoroughly. Cut into 1½-inch (approximately) squares. Yield: 48 cookies.

- Add any of the following: 1 cup miniature marshmallows, ½ cup maraschino cherries (drained and cut up), other nuts, cut up dried fruit (dates, apricots, raisins, or prunes), or a layer of ½ cup peanut butter mixed with 2 tbsp milk (to make it easier to spread).

ENRICHMENTS

- Children can make their own graham-cracker crumbs by placing crackers in a plastic bag and breaking them up by rolling them with a rolling pin. Have them comment on the changes in texture and consistency.
- Children can grate their own coconut: empty the water from a whole coconut by piercing its eyes with an ice pick (the teacher does this), and draining. (Be sure to have children taste the coconut water, as it is delicious.) Then whack the hard shell with a hammer. It should break up readily so you can peel it off with your fingers. The children can then grate the meat.
- When cutting, vary the shapes and sizes of the cookies as a practical lesson in mathematics.

Almost-Cool Cookies Mix 2 cups sugar, 2 tbsp cocoa, and 1 cup milk in a saucepan. Cook over low heat about 1 minute, stirring to dissolve the sugar thoroughly. Add ¼ cup butter, and continue to heat until it melts. Remove from heat, and stir in ½ cup peanut butter, 1 tsp vanilla extract, 2 cups uncooked rolled oats, and ½ tsp salt. Drop by spoonfuls onto wax paper. Yield: 48 cookies.

VARIATION

- A different version can be made the same way with these ingredients: 2 cups sugar, 3 tbsp cocoa, ½ cup (or 1 cube) margarine, pinch of salt, 1 cup shredded coconut, and 3 cups uncooked oats.

ENRICHMENTS

- Let the children grate their own coconut (above).
- Let the children make their own peanut butter (p. 68).
- Let the children crack and shell the nuts themselves.

- Use different kinds of sugar—brown, raw, or powdered. Point out the differences. Let the children taste and touch them all.

Uncooked Butter Frosting

Cream ½ cup butter or margarine in a bowl. Sift 4 cups (1 pound) powdered sugar onto wax paper, if necessary, to remove any lumps, and add 1 cup of the sugar to the creamed shortening. Add 1 egg yolk (optional), 1½ tsp vanilla extract, and 2 tbsp cream or milk. Gradually add the remaining sugar alternately with ¼ cup to ½ cup cream or milk (as needed, to make the frosting thick and creamy). This will cover two 9-inch layer cakes or 24 cupcakes.

VARIATIONS

- *Mocha.* Add 1 tbsp cocoa and 1 tsp instant coffee.
- *Orange.* Substitute thawed frozen orange juice concentrate for vanilla extract and cream or milk. You might also add 1 tbsp orange rind, 1 tsp grated lemon rind, or 1 tsp lemon juice.
- *Lemon.* Substitute thawed frozen lemonade concentrate for vanilla extract and cream or milk. You might also add 1 tsp grated lemon rind.
- *Chocolate Butter.* Add ¼ cup cocoa with the powdered sugar.
- *Fruit Icings.* Substitute fruit juice or pureed fruits (p. 59), such as peaches, apricots, Bing or maraschino cherries, prunes, pineapple, or nectarines, for the cream or milk. Use as much as needed to achieve the desired consistency for spreading.
- *Tinted Frosting.* Add a few drops of any food coloring.
- Use chocolate chips, butterscotch chips, chocolate shot, coconut, nonpareils, candy confetti, gumdrops, miniature marshmallows, or the like for decoration after the cake is iced.
- A sheet cake cut into sections can be decorated with chocolate chips to simulate dominoes. This is a good way to practice numbers while they eat. Each child can decorate a "domino."
- Frost ready-made cookies, animal crackers, graham crackers, cupcakes, or birthday cakes.
- Use as cement to paste together a quick graham-cracker house, a marshmallow house, a sugar-cube house, or a cookie house (p. 142).

- Make one batch with butter and one with margarine, and compare the two.
- Don't forget to tie in the color of any nearby holiday with your tinted frosting (orange and black for Halloween; red and green for Christmas; pastels for Easter; blue and white for Chanukah; autumn colors for Thanksgiving; red, white, and blue for Fourth of July or Flag Day).
- Have a color lesson by combining tints as you would tempera colors.
- Purchase a cake-decorating kit, and let the children make their own designs on a cake or on wax paper. Let them "write" their names with the writing tube.
- Buy chocolate Easter eggs, and let the children decorate them with frosting.

"Cool" Vanilla Ice-Cream

Beat 4 eggs in a bowl to blend. Add 2¼ cups sugar gradually, and continue to beat until very thick (the consistency of heavy cream). Add 5 cups milk, 4 cups heavy cream, 5 tsp vanilla extract, and ½ tsp salt. Mix thoroughly. Pour into 1-gallon freezer, and freeze as directed using rock salt and ice, or see p. 160. Remove dasher, allow children to scrape the ice-cream off it with their fingers and taste it. Either eat the ice-cream right away, at this soft stage, or cover the container of ice-cream with wax paper or foil, return it to the freezer, cover it with ice and salt, and allow it to harden and ripen for at least ½ hour. Yield: 4 quarts ice-cream.

Gelatin Desserts

Dissolve 3 ounces commercial gelatin dessert in 2 cups boiling water by stirring thoroughly in a bowl. Pour it into individual molds which have been rinsed in cold water and then lightly oiled, or into paper cups. Refrigerate until set. Yield: 8 servings.

To unmold when the gelatin is set, dip the mold into warm water about 5 seconds. Cover it with a plate, and turn it upside down, so gelatin falls out on the plate. If it doesn't work the first time, repeat.

VARIATIONS

- Dissolve flavored gelatin powder in 1 cup boiling water. Add 10 medium-size ice cubes.

Mix until ice is melted. Refrigerate. This sets more quickly than gelatin made by the method described above.

- Chill gelatin dessert until syrupy, and add any kind of fresh, frozen, or drained canned fruit, nuts, or vegetables. Do not use fresh pineapple, as it will prevent the gelatin from setting.
- Chill until syrupy, and then beat with a rotary eggbeater until the gelatin is double in volume. At this point, fold in a beaten egg white or 1 cup heavy cream, whipped, or 1 pint melted ice-cream.
- Unflavored gelatin may be used with fruit juices and sugar to make the same type of dessert. It might be especially valuable to make the two types of gelatin dessert at the same time to compare flavors. To make a gelatin dessert from scratch, dissolve an envelope of unflavored gelatin (1 tbsp) in ½ cup water. Mix, and let soften 5 minutes. Heat 1½ cups fruit or vegetable juice (or combination of juices or soft drinks). Pour over softened gelatin, and mix well. Set as above.
- Wipe top and bottom of a 20-ounce can of sliced pineapple with a damp cloth. Open one end, drain the juice, and save it to make gelatin dessert as above. Pour a mixed, prepared gelatin dessert into the can with the pineapple slices still in. Cover, and refrigerate until set. Open the other end of the can, and push the whole mixture through the open end, using the metal bottom for a pusher, onto a plate. To serve, cut in between the pineapple slices. (There are 10 slices in this size can.)

ENRICHMENTS

- Point out how the gelatin melts after it has been dissolved in hot water and how it firms up when it is chilled.
- Point out the change in texture when the mixture is beaten in the syrupy stage. Discuss the change in volume when air is beaten into the mixture.
- Use a variety of molds, such as rounds, animals, and melon shapes.

Finger Jello Put 3 tbsp plain gelatin in 1 cup cold water in a small bowl. Mix thoroughly, and let soften 5 minutes. Put 2 packages commercial flavored gelatin dessert in a large bowl with 2 cups boiling water (or 1 cup boiling water and 10 ice cubes), and stir until dissolved. Add softened plain gelatin to this mixture, and stir thoroughly. Pour into an 8″ × 8″ pan. Refrigerate until set. It sets up very rapidly (about 15 minutes). Cut into 1-inch cubes. This gelatin will not melt and can be eaten by hand. (It can be packed in lunch boxes and taken on a picnic without melting.) Yield: sixty-four 1-inch cubes.

VARIATIONS

- Use different colors and flavors.
- Use molds of different shapes.
- Add grated carrots, chopped celery, or any well drained fruit or vegetable.
- Cut into very small pieces, and add to fruit salad, or use as a topping for puddings.
- Make several flavors, and cut them into half-inch squares. Pile into dessert dishes, and serve as a dessert or snack. An appropriate name is *Jello Jewels*.
- For "buried treasure," pour ungelled Finger Jello into individual glass custard cups or other molds. Add a shrimp, a radish, an olive, fresh mint, a marshmallow, a washed flower (see pp. 63-64 on poisonous flowers), parsley, a cherry tomato, a mushroom, or any other food that looks attractive. When set, unmold. The children can handle the jelly with buried treasure because of its unusual firmness.
- If you do not wish to use commercial gelatin desserts, make your own flavored gelatin dessert as on p. 88.
- Pour into ice-cube trays, and insert dividers. When removed, Finger Jello is automatically sectioned.

ENRICHMENTS

- Point out the differences in texture and firmness between this and ordinary gelatin dessert.
- Point out the different colors and flavors of gelatins, and talk about how we associate particular colors with flavors such as orange, lemon, lime, strawberry, cherry, and raspberry.

- Unmold a whole undivided pan of Finger Jello on a board. Let the children cut out different shapes freehand or with cookie cutters.

Raspadas or Snow Cones

Crush ice in an electric ice crusher, or scrape it into very fine particles by hand, and pack it into paper cups. Pour commercial fruit syrup or frozen fruit-juice concentrate (thawed) over the top. Eat immediately with spoons. Half a cup of crushed ice and 2 tbsp syrup make one snow cone.

VARIATIONS

- Dribble ¼ cup sweetened condensed milk over the ice with the fruit syrup.
- Insert sticks into the snow cones. Freeze. Turn them out of the cups, and eat them like popsicles.
- Use various shapes and various sizes of paper cups. Compare.

ENRICHMENTS

- Talk about cold and how it feels.
- Let the children taste the ice before adding syrup or juice. Point out how the ice melts and becomes water.
- Discuss solid, liquid, and gas states of water. If possible, boil the meltwater from the ice, and discuss how the steam forms.
- Let the children make snowballs or snowmen from the crushed ice.
- Let the children crush ice in a heavy plastic bag with a hammer. Be sure to put it in a strong plastic bag and hammer it on a wooden board. (This is a valid experience by itself.)
- Visit your local iceman, if you have one, and ask him to tell about his business, or try to get a picture of an old ice wagon. Point out how our customs have changed since mechanical refrigeration was invented.
- Explain the differences between iceboxes, refrigerators, and freezers.
- Let the children mold the ice, alone, in cups or in gelatin molds. Freeze them, and then unmold them. (Do not fill too full, as water expands when it freezes.) You can also vary the

molds by partially filling them with water, freezing them, and then putting in a flower (see p. 62) or a colorful food like a slice of carrot or fruit. Fill the rest of the mold with water, and refreeze. When unmolded, "buried treasure" shines through.
- Make popsicles by filling paper cups about ⅔ full with punch or fruit juice. Freeze until it is firm enough to hold a stick inserted in the center. Refreeze. Unmold to eat.

Play-and-Eat Fondant Cream ½ cup softened butter or margarine in a bowl. Add ½ cup light corn syrup, ½ tsp salt, 1 tsp vanilla extract, and 4 cups powdered sugar. Mix well, using hands, if necessary. Divide into equal portions, one for each child. Allow the children to knead the mixture with their hands on wax paper until well blended and smooth.

Then let them use it like clay, forming it into shapes, rolling it out, cutting it, stamping it with pattern blocks, or rolling it into marble-size balls. They can discover eating it on their own. Yield: 4 cups, or 8 portions.

VARIATIONS
- Use flavorings other than vanilla (peppermint, almond, anise, strawberry, orange, lemon, banana, and wintergreen are strong and should be used in smaller quantities than vanilla — about ½ tsp). For a richer flavor, use ½ tsp vanilla and ½ tsp of another flavor.
- *Chocolate Logs.* Add 2 tbsp cocoa. Shape into rolls about ½ inch in diameter and 2 inches long. Roll in chocolate shot.
- A variety of food colors can be added while the fondant is being mixed. Combine colors to show the development of secondary colors (it is fun for the children to make their favorite colors). This would mean adding the color while the children are kneading their individual portions. The color can also be streaked, to give another effect.
- Textural variations can be achieved by rolling the fondant in chopped nuts, shredded coconut, chocolate sprinkles, nonpareils, melted chocolate, butterscotch bits, or any other cake decorations.

- Stress the difference between this special "clay," which can be tasted, and ordinary clay, which is not for eating.
- Should the children wish to build structures or designs, forms, shapes, animals, or people, you should encourage them. But refrain from imposing high standards of accomplishment by making examples yourself. The children should be allowed to experiment freely.
- The children can undertake a group project by making a candy house for Christmas or the witch's house in Hansel and Gretel with this fondant. Make the parts of a base house of cardboard. Make bricks, roof tiles, windows, doors, trees, and flowers from fondant, and attach them to the cardboard base pieces with a paste made of ½ cup powdered sugar and enough water to moisten it. Then fasten all the pieces together. This will be very attractive to ants, so store it in a safe place.

4

Cool Cooking with Heat

RECIPES THAT USE A HEAT SOURCE

Since cooking is generally thought to involve the use of heat, it is important to provide children with experiences in this area. For this, we have selected some of the best-loved favorites that have proved especially successful in exposing children to the wide world of cooking. We have included far more material than you will need, in order to present you with a large variety of possibilities from which to select whichever are most comfortable for you to work with.

Surprisingly, these recipes do not require much cooking equipment. If your school does not have a regular range, you can supply such simple equipment as an electric element, an electric skillet or saucepan, or a portable toaster-oven.

The recipes appear in the form of lesson plans, so they can be incorporated into the curriculum easily. For some of them you may want to do a little of the cooking beforehand. This will not detract from the effectiveness of the lessons, and it can cut them down to a reasonable time, if your time is limited. The symbol ☂ identifies operations the teacher should do.

A final caution—do not be too concerned about the quality of the finished products, because the important thing is the children's involvement in the activities. It would be sad for children to be deprived of taking part in this meaningful life activity because a teacher was needlessly afraid of not producing perfect results.

How to Treat a Good Egg

2 years–kindergarten
Cooking times (hen's eggs):
soft, 3 minutes; medium, 5 minutes; hard, 20;
other eggs, time varies with size

soft- and hard-cooked eggs–hen (brown and white eggs), duck, turkey, quail, or whatever

Equipment
large saucepan with lid
slotted spoon
bowl

1. Pour a large quantity of water into a saucepan (enough to cover eggs with 1 inch of water). Bring to a boil. ☺
2. Slip eggs, preferably at room temperature, from a slotted spoon into the water.
3. Cover the saucepan. Turn heat to simmer, and time the eggs (for hen's eggs, 3 minutes for soft-cooked, 5 minutes for medium-cooked, 20 minutes for hard-cooked; hard-cook all other eggs, varying the time according to size). Note: Do not *boil* eggs, as it makes the whites rubbery, tough, and tasteless and forms a green ring around the yolk.
4. When done, remove the eggs with a slotted spoon to a bowl of cold water. This will make them easier to handle and peel and will stop the cooking.

To peel a hard-cooked egg, when it is cool enough to handle, give the egg a sharp rap with a tablespoon, to crack the shell. Return it to cold water, and cool it completely. Peel by starting at the large end. Some very fresh eggs are difficult to peel, so don't get discouraged. This method works well for most eggs!

To peel soft-cooked eggs, crack them in the middle crosswise with a kitchen knife. Break them in halves, and scoop them out with a teaspoon. Another technique is to set the eggs in eggcups (or in double sections cut from an egg carton), crack the top section and remove a small portion of the shell. Then eat from the shell.

- Hard-cooked eggs make excellent snacks, so keep some in the refrigerator. Slice in halves, quarters, or circles, allowing ¼ to ½ egg per child accompanied by half a slice of buttered whole-wheat bread.
- *Stuffed (or Deviled) Eggs.* Cut hard-cooked eggs in half, lengthwise or crosswise. Remove yolks, and mash them with a fork. Add any combination of seasonings, such as salt, pepper, mayonnaise, sour cream, mustard, ketchup, cottage cheese, relish, chopped pickles, chili sauce, chopped celery, or (as a special experience) caviar (explain that fish have eggs, too). Fill hollows in the egg whites with mashed, seasoned egg yolk. Sprinkle with a dash of paprika for color, or top with a slice of pickle or green pepper or a sprig of parsley.
- *Custard.* Break 3 eggs into a mixing bowl, and mix well with an eggbeater. Beat in ½ cup sugar, ⅛ tsp salt, and ½ tsp nutmeg. Stir in 2 cups milk and 1 tsp vanilla extract. Pour into 8 greased custard cups. Set cups into a baking pan in a 350° oven. Pour boiling water into the pan almost to the top of the custard. Bake 45 minutes or until a table knife inserted into the custard comes out clean. Serve warm or cold.
- *Colored Eggs (Without Shells).* Remove shells from hard-cooked eggs (see above), and rinse with cold water. Immerse in beet juice until desired shade is achieved (or overnight). Or immerse in water tinted with a small amount of vegetable food coloring until desired shade is achieved. Remove from time to time so children can observe color changes. Make two-toned eggs by dipping each end in a different-color dye.
- *Colored Eggs (with Shells).* Dilute tablet or liquid food coloring in ¼ cup water in glass custard cups, to allow children to observe the changes. Easter egg kits come with metal egg holders. If you do not have one, use a metal spoon, as the dye will stain a wooden spoon or

children's fingers. Before dipping hard-cooked eggs in dye, the children may want to put their names or designs on the shells with wax crayons, candle ends, or paraffin. Dip as above. They can also make two-toned eggs as above. This experience can be used as a lesson on color by dipping eggs first into one of the primary colors (red, yellow, or blue) and then into one of the other primary colors, to produce secondary colors. They can also marbleize eggs by cracking eggs slightly by rolling them on a hard surface and dyeing as usual. Remove from the dye, wipe them dry with a paper towel, and peel. The results are a marbled design on the inside egg surface.

- *Egg Salad.* Chop hard-cooked eggs. Add chopped celery, chopped onions, chopped green peppers, pickle relish, chopped leftover vegetables, chopped ham or chicken, chopped salami, or cold cuts (or any combination). Add enough mayonnaise or salad dressing to hold everything together. Salt to taste. Serve on a lettuce leaf as a salad. Or use as a sandwich spread on bread or crackers. Or stuff in celery as a snack.
- *Scrambled Eggs.* (These are good for lunch or midmorning snack.) For each child allow 1 egg, 1 tbsp milk, and ⅛ tsp salt. Beat egg until well mixed. Beat in salt and milk. Melt 1 tbsp margarine in a skillet on low to medium heat (300°). Pour beaten eggs into the heated pan. As mixture cooks, stir with a wooden spoon until creamy curds form throughout. Serve immediately. If left in the pan, egg will continue to cook. Do not overcook.

  If desired, add precooked bacon, sausage, or ham before serving. Or, tint the eggs with green food coloring and serve them while reading Dr. Seuss's *Green Eggs and Ham* (New York: Random House, Inc., Beginner Books, 1960).

ENRICHMENTS

- Buy fertilized eggs and incubate them (see p. 75).
- Buy a variety of eggs such as chicken (white and brown), duck, goose, or whatever is available, and compare size, color, texture, and so forth.

- Collect pictures of birds—nests, feathers, baby birds, birds incubating eggs, wild birds, tame birds, and so on. Make a "bird book" with any that are available. Glue the pictures onto shirt cardboards, make holes in the tops, and hold the pages together with two key rings.
- Charts of the internal development of the egg appear in biology books. Also check your library for other books or stories on birds. *What's Inside the Egg?* by Mae Garelic (Reading, Mass.: Addison-Wesley Publishing Co., Inc., 1955) is a delightful picture story of the hatching of an egg. Another version is *What's Inside* (New York: Scholastic Book Services, 1970).
- Make collages with broken eggshells (colored and white) by gluing them on construction paper or cardboard.
- Demonstrate how to separate eggs. (1) Crack an egg by hitting it in the center crosswise with a table knife. Pull the shell apart (over a bowl) with both hands, carefully transferring the egg yolk back and forth from one half of the shell to the other, allowing the egg white to drain into the bowl, until the egg yolk is completely alone in the shell. (2) Younger children can do this by cracking the egg and pouring the entire contents into the top of a funnel that has been placed in a tall glass. The white will drain through, leaving the yolk in the funnel. Shake gently if necessary.

  Use whites to make Boom-Meringue Kisses (p. 155). Use yolks for scrambled eggs (above), eggnog, or custard (p. 95), or add them to cakes, puddings, and cookies.
- Take the children to market to purchase eggs for your cooking project.
- Visit a poultry farm if possible.
- Collect feathers of all kinds for collages.
- Use egg cartons for: art projects, storing small items, classifying objects, and separating (by sizes, shapes, colors) for small-muscle development.

Meat-Loaf Lollipops

1½ pounds ground beef
8 ounces canned tomato
sauce with cheese
1 egg
½ cup crushed pretzels,
crackers, or bread crumbs
2 tsp instant minced onion
12 pickle slices

Equipment

12 wooden skewers, 5 or 6
inches long
large bowl
wooden spoon
12-well muffin tin, lightly
oiled
cookie sheet covered with
aluminum foil
paring knife

Yield 12 servings

1. Preheat oven to 350°. ☝
2. Combine beef, ¼ cup tomato sauce, egg, crumbs, and onions in the bowl.
3. Mix lightly, but well, with the wooden spoon.
4. Press mixture firmly into 12 medium-sized, greased muffin-tin wells.
5. Place muffin pan on foil-covered cookie sheet to keep the oven clean.
6. Bake 20 minutes.
7. Pour off fat into a wide-mouthed can or milk carton by tilting the muffin tin carefully. Spoon remaining tomato sauce into individual wells. ☝
8. Bake 5 minutes longer.
9. Carefully remove meat from wells by inserting a paring knife between meat and muffin tin and gently loosening the meat.
10. Top each with a pickle slice, and then push a wooden skewer into the pickle and firmly into the meat to form a lollipop. These may be served hot or chilled.

VARIATIONS

- Show the children how to make crumbs by putting crackers or pretzels in a heavy plastic bag, sealing the bag with a wire closure, and rolling over the bag with a rolling pin.
- Use a blender to make bread crumbs from fresh or dried bread.
- Use dry cereal, oatmeal, or wheat germ in place of bread crumbs.
- Use skim milk powder for added nutritional value (about ¼ cup).
- Use tuna fish instead of meat (two 6-ounce cans).
- Use ground lamb with pine nuts for a Mediterranean touch.
- Use chicken or turkey, chopped fine. (Bless those leftovers!)

- Try different spices and seasonings, such as mint with lamb, and oregano, parsley, cumin, garlic, or soy sauce. Use small amounts, as most children do not like highly spiced food. Let the children smell each new ingredient and learn its name. Use about ½ tsp for this amount of meat. Garlic powder should be used in a lesser quantity (about ¼ tsp).

ENRICHMENTS

- Take the children to visit a butcher shop. If possible, arrange ahead of time to visit the back where the meat is stored as carcasses. Let the children buy the meat that will be used in the cooking lesson and watch the butcher grind it.
- Try to visit a butcher who will explain how meat is stored, the cutting tools he uses, packaging, and the necessity for cleanliness and careful handling.
- Show the children pictures of animals used for meat in various places around the world, such as cattle, sheep, hogs, deer, rabbits, llamas, buffalo, moose, poultry (wild and domestic), bears, squirrels, and assorted fish and shellfish.
- Explain the importance of sanitation and proper care of meat. Children are not too young to understand that meat is an excellent medium for bacterial growth and, as such, must be handled properly to prevent spoilage.
- Older children may be interested in viewing actual internal organs, such as the heart, lungs, and kidneys of animals, but *only if the teacher feels comfortable in so doing*. Check your library for reference books if you want to show pictures.
- Explain that almost the total animal is used in many cases. Hides are used for leather, bones for gelatin, horns for buttons. Point out objects in the room made of leather, such as shoes, handbags, wallets, belts, jackets, pants, and coats.

Hamburger Toast

*8 slices of bread toasted on
one side or 4 hamburger
buns*
*mustard, catsup, or pickle
relish (optional)*
1 pound lean ground beef
8 slices of cheese (optional)
salt
pepper

Equipment

wax paper
table knife
baking sheet or broiler pan

Yield 8 full servings or
32 snack strips

1. Preheat broiler to 450° (after removing broiler pan). ⊕
2. If desired, spread untoasted side of bread or buns with mustard or catsup or pickle relish.
3. Divide beef into 8 equal portions.
4. Spread toast or buns with a thin, even layer of beef, spreading meat to cover the edges.
5. Season with salt and pepper.
6. Place on baking sheet or broiler pan, and put pan 2 or 3 inches below the broiler. ⊕
7. Broil about 5 minutes, or to taste.
8. If desired, add a slice of cheese to each for the last 30 seconds.
9. Serve as open-face sandwiches, or cut into 4 strips each for finger food.

VARIATIONS

- Substitute tuna for the hamburger. Or, try ground lamb, ground cooked ham, ground veal, or ground chicken.
- "Hide" a cooked vegetable under the meat.
- Use lunch meat with cheese.

ENRICHMENTS

(See Meat-Loaf Lollipops, p. 98.)

Pig in a Blanket

*hotdogs (1 per child) or
cocktail hotdogs (2 or 3 per
child)*
*refrigerator biscuits (2 per
regular hotdog)*
mustard or relish (optional)
*small inch-wide slices of
cheddar, Monterey Jack,
or Swiss cheese (optional)*

Equipment
cutting board
table knives
cookie sheet

Yield 2 or 3 "pigs" per child

1. Preheat oven to 375°.
2. Cut hotdogs in half crosswise. With cocktail hotdogs, omit this step.
3. Separate biscuits. Flatten each one with your palm so it can be rolled around half a full-size hotdog.
4. Spread each flattened biscuit with mustard, relish, or cheese, if desired.
5. Roll each half hotdog in a biscuit.
6. Place, seam side down, on a cookie sheet about 1 inch apart.
7. Bake 10 minutes, or until brown on top.

VARIATIONS

- Slit hotdog the long way, and insert a piece of cheese before wrapping it in biscuit.
- Substitute a rolled slice of bologna, a sausage, a carrot stick, a piece of squash, cucumber, pickle, or other firm vegetable for the hotdog.
- A piece of fresh fruit sprinkled with cinnamon and sugar, such as a slice of fresh apple, may also be used to fill biscuits.
- Make your own biscuits (see p. 121), or use our pretzel dough recipe (p. 117) instead of the canned biscuits.

ENRICHMENTS

- Take a field trip to a hotdog or sausage factory or a food market.
- Examine the variety of sausages in a supermarket. Buy some for tasting.
- Discuss spices used in hotdogs and sausages, such as salt, pepper, paprika, bay leaf, oregano, fennel seed, and pistachio nuts. Buy samples, and let the children examine, taste, feel, and smell them.

- Buy a whole salami, and hang it in the room. Watch the casing wither as the salami dries out. Taste at intervals. Keep cut surface covered with foil. The heavy spicing inhibits the growth of bacteria, which keeps the salami from spoiling like most meats. Uncut, you can keep a salami three months; after it is cut, you should use it within two weeks.

Pizza Individuals

2 years–kindergarten
Baking time: 15 minutes

6 English muffins,
or 12 pilot crackers,
or 1 package refrigerator
biscuits
8 ounces tomato paste
½ tsp. each, sweet basil,
oregano, salt
¼ tsp pepper
½ pound American cheese,
Monterey Jack cheese, or
mozzarella
½ cup Parmesan cheese
6 slices salami
½ cup chopped green onions
olive oil
mushrooms (optional)
olives (optional)

1. Preheat oven to 450°.
2. Split English muffins, or roll out biscuits to a 3-inch diameter each. Arrange them or pilot crackers on a cookie sheet.
3. Put tomato paste into the bowl with basil, oregano, salt, and pepper. Mix well.
4. Spread on muffins, biscuits, or crackers.
5. Cover with meat, cheese, onion, and other desired toppings.
6. Drizzle with olive oil.
7. Bake 15 to 20 minutes, or until cheese melts and base is brown.

VARIATIONS

- Anchovies, Italian sausage, pepperoni, chopped bell pepper, pork sausage (cooked), may be added to topping.
- Make your own pizza base, using Bread Sculpture Dough (p. 130).
- Make a large pizza in a circular pizza pan or a cookie sheet by patting Bread Sculpture Dough or refrigerator biscuits to fit the pan. Follow Steps 3–7, above.

Equipment

cookie sheet
mixing spoons
measuring cups
measuring spoons
knife
cutting board
spatula
bowl

Yield 12 pizzas

ENRICHMENTS

- Talk about Italy and about pizza as a traditional food.
- Take the children on a field trip to a pizza parlor.
- Set out a variety of toppings, and let the children make their own original pizzas.
- Using fresh tomatoes, let the children make their own tomato sauce. Peel the tomatoes, and cook over low heat until very thick.
- Make an Italian dinner. Include spaghetti, meatballs, minestrone soup, Italian water ice or spumoni ice-cream, Italian cookies.
- Play Italian records. Learn an Italian song.
- Get a picture of an Italian flag. Discuss its meaning.
- Invite an Italian visitor.
- Show them a map of Italy, shaped like a boot.
- Show pictures of Italian folk costumes.
- Visit an Italian store.

Spaghetti, Macaroni, Noodles, and Other Pasta

2 years–kindergarten
Cooking time: 15 minutes

1 ounce pasta per person
2 ounces per person heated canned spaghetti sauce
salt
grated Parmesan cheese

Equipment

large pot to hold at least 4 quarts of water for each pound of spaghetti
colander or strainer
large fork
serving bowl or platter
large spoon

1. Fill the pot with water, and bring it to a boil.
2. Add 1 tbsp salt for every 4 quarts of water.
3. Add pasta slowly, so boiling does not stop. Be sure pasta is submerged.
4. Boil rapidly until pasta is tender (about 15 minutes, or according to package). Test by pressing a piece of pasta against the side of the pot. It should be easy to cut with the fork.
5. Drain quickly by pouring the pasta and water into the colander in the sink. (Be careful to stand out of the way of the steam.)
6. Stop the cooking by running cold water through the pasta in the colander. Then pour pasta into a serving dish.
7. Add heated spaghetti sauce. (Sauce is too complicated to make and takes too long for the attention span of preschool children.)
8. Top with grated Parmesan cheese.

VARIATIONS

- Vary the sauces, trying cheese sauce, meat sauce, clam sauce, melted butter and cheese, and tomato sauce mixed with vegetables.
- Buy spinach noodles, and prepare them in the same manner.
- Macaroni Salad: Cook and cool elbow macaroni. Add mayonnaise, chopped onion, chopped bell peppers, salt, and pepper to taste. Chill, and serve.
- *Baked Macaroni and Cheese.* ¼ pound macaroni (cooked); 1½ cups milk; 1 tsp prepared mustard (optional); ¼ pound grated cheddar; ½ cup bread crumbs or crushed corn chips or potato chips. Mix macaroni, milk, mustard, and cheese in a bowl. Pour into a buttered baking dish, top with crumbs, and bake at 400° for 15 minutes. Yield: 10 child-size servings.

- Buy different shapes of pasta. Cook as directed, and serve with any sauce.
- Make lasagna according to directions on the package.

- Visit an Italian store to see the different shapes of pasta.
- Make a collage of pastas of various shapes.
- Layer pastas of different shapes in a large glass jar. Pack tightly so they won't move.
- If possible, invite a parent who knows how to make noodles to give a demonstration. (Or you may do this yourself.)
- Discuss the difference in volume between cooked and uncooked pasta. Explain how it absorbs the water and becomes heavier and also occupies more space.

FRUITS AND VEGETABLES

Potatoes

2 years–kindergarten
Cooking time: 30–45 minutes

potatoes
salt
water

Equipment

large pot with lid
slotted spoon
fork
table knife

1. Select potatoes of uniform size if they are to be cooked whole, so they all will cook in an equal length of time.
2. Clean potatoes that will be cooked in the skin, by scrubbing them with a stiff brush under running water.
3. Remove all bruised sections, and cut out the eyes with a small knife.
4. If potatoes are peeled or sliced, cover them with cold water until all are ready to cook, to prevent discoloration.
5. To cook potatoes in their skins, cover them with water. Bring water to a boil. Reduce heat, and simmer until the potatoes are easily pierced to the center with a fork. This may take anywhere from 30 to 45 minutes, depending on the size of the potatoes. (Large potatoes may be cut in half before cooking, to reduce the time.) When done, drain water. When cool enough to handle, peel with a table knife. Season, if you like, with salt, pepper, and butter.

VARIATIONS

- *Mashed Potatoes.* For every four potatoes (cooked, drained, and peeled), add ½ cup heated milk and 2 tbsp butter or margarine. Mash with a potato masher until smooth. Add salt and pepper to taste.

- *Riced Potatoes*. Force boiled, peeled potatoes through a potato ricer. Season to taste with salt, pepper, and butter.
- *Potato Salad*. Cube or slice cooked potatoes. Allow ¼ to ½ potato for each child. Add any of the following ingredients in any desired amount—sliced hard-cooked eggs, chopped raw onions, green onions, pickle relish, chopped bell pepper, bacon bits, chopped celery, and chopped parsley. Mix with any of the following dressings: French, cooked, mayonnaise, or mayonnaise and sour cream mixed. Use from 2 tbsp to 4 tbsp dressing for every 4 potatoes. Salt and pepper to taste. Chill or serve warm.
- *Baked Potatoes*. Preheat oven to 425°. Select baking potatoes (Idaho russets preferred) of uniform size. Scrub with a stiff brush under running water. Skins may be lightly brushed with oil. Arrange on a baking sheet, and cut a slit in the top of each potato with a knife, to allow the steam to escape. Bake 1 hour, or until easily pierced with a fork. Add butter and salt to taste. Yogurt or sour cream can be used in place of butter.
- *Twice-Baked Potatoes*. Bake potatoes as above. Cut in half lengthwise, and scoop contents into a bowl, being careful not to break the skins. Mash with a fork, add butter, hot milk, salt, and pepper. Beat until smooth and fluffy. Return to shells. Arrange on a baking sheet. Bake at 425° for 15 minutes, or until lightly browned. Potatoes may also be topped with shredded cheddar before baking.
- *Potato Latkes (Pancakes)*. 3 potatoes, washed and peeled, 2 slightly beaten eggs, 1 tbsp flour, 1 tbsp milk, ½ tsp salt. Grate potatoes into a mixing bowl. Add eggs, flour, milk, and salt. Mix thoroughly but quickly, keeping mixture light. If batter is not thick enough to hold its shape on the griddle, add flour, a teaspoon at a time. Heat griddle, and grease it lightly with oil. Test for correct temperature by dripping a drop of water on the griddle. (It should dance when the griddle is hot enough.) Drop batter by tablespoonfuls onto the griddle. Cook on one side until lightly brown, turn, and cook on the other side until done. Remove

to a plate, spread with butter, and serve with traditional sour cream and applesauce. (Jam, jelly, or other canned fruits may also be served with the potatoes.)

- Place an unpeeled potato in a glass jar half covered with water, so the children can observe the top and the roots as they start to grow. Add water as needed to keep the potato covered halfway. Choose a white potato, a sweet potato, or a yam. This makes a beautiful plant that will last indefinitely.
- Buy a variety of potatoes. (This includes different varieties of white potatoes, sweet potatoes, and yams.) Taste them all in the raw state. Cook, and compare again for flavor, color, texture, and appearance.
- *Potato Prints.* Cut a large potato in half crosswise, and cut a design into the center. Dip that face into tempera paint, and press it onto paper at random. Any other root vegetable will work as well. Green or red bell peppers or oranges or lemons also make interesting designs when cut in half and used as stamps.
- Plant a potato garden by cutting a potato into 1½-inch cubes, each containing an eye. Plant about 4 inches below the ground and about 12 inches to 18 inches apart. Keep well watered. When green tops flower, potatoes can be dug up and eaten. These are new potatoes. When green tops wither, potatoes are mature.
- Check your songbook for songs on potatoes.

Vegetable Soup

½ cup diced potatoes
1 cup green peas
½ cup sliced carrots
¼ cup sliced celery
2 tbsp chopped onions
4 cups boiling water
¼ cup tomato juice
*   or 1 fresh tomato*
3 bouillon cubes (chicken
*   or beef)*
salt and pepper to taste
¼ cup margarine

Equipment

4-quart pot
cutting board
knives
vegetable peeler
wooden spoon
measuring cups
measuring spoons

Yield 1½ quarts, or 12 half-cup
servings

1. Peel and cut up all vegetables, and place them in a large pot.
2. Pour in water, and bring it to a boil.
3. Lower heat, cover, and simmer 30 minutes.
4. Add bouillon cubes, stir gently to dissolve, and simmer 15 minutes longer.
5. Add margarine, stirring until it is melted.
6. Taste for salt, and add salt only if necessary.
7. Add ¼ tsp pepper, if desired.
8. Simmer another 10 minutes until everything is well blended.

VARIATIONS

- Add any leftover cooked vegetables in the last 5 minutes of cooking.
- Substitute seasonal vegetables.
- Cooked fish, chicken, or meat may be added in the last 5 minutes.
- Cooked noodles or cooked rice may be added in the last 5 minutes of cooking.
- Toast bread, spread it with margarine or garlic butter, cut it into rectangles of any size, and float them on the individual servings.
- Garnish soup with grated Parmesan cheese before serving.
- Substitute any vegetable water for plain water in the recipe.
- Let soup cool slightly, and whirl it in a blender for a pureed soup. Reheat.

ENRICHMENTS

- Start a vegetable garden to use in your soup someday (see p. 64).
- Start a vegetable scrapbook by cutting pictures out of magazines, mounting them on shirt cardboards, and fastening them together with key rings.

- Have the children bring in pictures of different kinds of soups.
- See your library for a copy of the story "Stone Soup."
- Buy a variety of canned soups, and compare.
- Buy packaged soups, and compare.
- Buy chicken or beef bouillon cubes, and reconstitute them.
- Create a new soup by mixing 2 or 3 canned soups.
- *Experimental Soup.* Have the children tell you what they want in their soup, and make it!

Applesauce and Other Fruit Sauces

2 years–kindergarten
Cooking time: 30 minutes

1 medium-size apple for each serving (use tart apples that break up on cooking, such as Pippin or Gravenstein)
sugar, about ½ tbsp for each serving, to taste

1. Wash apples, and polish them with paper towels (for fun).
2. Cut into quarters, but do not core or peel. (Skins add to the flavor.)
3. Add about 1 inch of water to the saucepan, and bring the water to a boil.
4. Add apples and simmer, covered, about 30 minutes, or until they can be mashed against the side of the pan easily. (This cooking can be done by the teacher out of school hours.)
5. Cool, and allow children to put the apples through the food mill, sieve, colander, or ricer.
6. Discard skins and cores.
7. Add sugar to taste. Brown sugar, raw sugar, or honey can also be used.

Have one of the children serve applesauce to the others.

Equipment

*food mill, colander, sieve,
    or ricer*
cutting board
paring knives
*saucepan (Pyrex is pre-
    ferred if you cook in
    school, so children can
    see what is going on) or
    electric saucepan*
*hot plate (if nonelectric
    saucepan is used)*
wooden spoon
paper towels

Yield 2 servings per medium
    apple

VARIATIONS

- Add food coloring.
- Add cinnamon, to taste.
- Dissolve cinnamon red-hots in boiling water. Then add them to the apples for a pretty color and an unusual flavor. Use about 2 tbsp candy and ⅓ cup water for about 12 apples.
- Serve on buttered bread, toast, or crackers for a snack.
- Use other fruits—apricots, peaches, nectarines, prunes, berries, or pears—instead of apples.
- Canned fruit can be used by skipping the cooking and simply putting it through the food mill.
- Sauces can be made by putting cooked or canned fruit, juice, and sugar in a blender. Blend until smooth.
- To eliminate Step 5, peel and core apples before cooking.

ENRICHMENTS

- Use this lesson as a starting point to discuss the planting, watering, fertilizing, spraying, harvesting, and marketing of fruits. Use photographs to illustrate.
- Discuss color, flavor, texture, and aroma of raw fruits, and compare with those of cooked fruits.
- Point out the physical changes that take place in cooking because of the application of heat.
- Discuss what temperature is. Use a candy thermometer if you have one. Remind the children they have their temperatures taken, too.
- Review measuring volume and time, and note and discuss changes in the volume of fruit and liquid with cooking.
- Have children listen to bubbling sounds when the fruit is boiling, and ask them to describe what they hear. Suggest that they imitate the bubbling sound. Have them pretend they are bubbles and create a "dance of the bubbles" to the rhythm of the drum.

BREADS AND THEIR FRIENDLY RELATIONS

Easy Bread and Rolls*

2 years–kindergarten
Baking times: small loaves, 25 minutes;
average loaves, 40 minutes; rolls, 20 minutes

½ cup lukewarm water
1 package dry yeast
1 tbsp sugar
¼ cup powdered milk
2 cups unsifted all-purpose
  flour
1 tsp salt
2 tbsp soft butter or
  margarine
1 egg, slightly beaten
salad oil

1. Preheat oven to 400°. ♁
2. Place yeast in warm water in a small bowl, and stir until dissolved.
3. Add sugar and milk powder, and mix. Allow to stand about 10 minutes. If yeast is active, the mixture will be frothy.
4. Add the egg and 1 cup flour, and beat with a wooden spoon 2 minutes.
5. Add salt and softened fat and half the remaining flour. Mix well.
6. Turn out mixture on floured board, and knead about 10 minutes, until the dough is well blistered and its surface is satiny.
7. Place in a large, lightly greased bowl, and turn dough over, to grease on all sides.
8. Cover well with wax paper, plastic wrap, or a damp dish towel, and allow to rise in a warm place (such as a gas oven with a pilot light) until it is double in bulk. (This should take about ½ hour.)

*Note: Bread or rolls may be made in two stages if you don't have time for the whole project at once. Punch down the dough after the first rising, flatten it, wrap it securely in plastic wrap or foil, and refrigerate. When you want to begin again, remove it from the refrigerator, and allow it to come to room temperature before shaping.

Equipment

measuring cups
measuring spoons
large bowl
small bowl
wooden mixing spoon
breadboard
*2 loaf pans or a baking
   sheet, greased*
fork
spatula
wax paper
cooling rack

Yield 2 small or 1 average loaf
of bread, or 12 rolls

9. Punch down in bowl with your fist. Knead dough again in the bowl about 2 minutes.
10. Dough is now ready to be shaped into loaves of bread (for rolls, see Step 17).
11. *To Make Bread.* To make either 2 small loaves or 1 average loaf, roll dough out lightly on floured board and fold into thirds. Cut in half for small loaves.
12. Place in greased loaf pans, seam side down.
13. Brush the top with oil, using a pastry brush.
14. Let rise until double in bulk, about 15 minutes.
15. Bake about 25 minutes for the small loaves, 40 minutes for an average loaf, or until nicely browned.
16. Cool in pan on a rack 5 minutes; then remove from pan and continue cooling.
17. *To Make Rolls.* Divide dough into 12 pieces, roll it between your palms, and shape in uniform balls.
    a. Place them on a lightly greased baking sheet, and brush the tops with melted shortening.
    b. Let rise 15 minutes, or until double in bulk.
    c. Bake 20 minutes, or until nicely browned.
    d. Cool on rack.

VARIATIONS

- Substitute any of the following for half the white flour: whole-wheat flour (graham flour); rye flour; soy flour; oatmeal.
- Add 1 tsp mace, cardamom, or cinnamon, or ½ tsp nutmeg.
- At Step 11, sprinkle dough with a mixture of 2 tbsp sugar, 1 tsp cinnamon, and ½ tsp nutmeg. Nuts may also be added at that point. Roll up, and proceed as before.
- Add 1 tsp grated lemon or orange rind at Step 4.
- Add ½ cup grated cheddar or American cheese after Step 5.

- Add ¼ cup of any chopped candied fruit after Step 5.
- Add between ¼ cup and ½ cup chopped dates after Step 5.
- *Monkey Bread.* (1) Grease a round 1-quart casserole. (2) Pull off 1-inch rounds of dough, and let the children roll them between *clean* hands to make balls. Dip in melted butter, and pile into greased casserole. (3) Let rise 30 minutes. (4) Bake about 40 minutes, or until lightly browned. (5) To serve, pull off in sections and eat.
- Rolls can be made from any bread dough in as many shapes as you can think of.
- *The Letters and Numbers Thing.* We hope that by now you realize you can make letters, numbers—any shape you want—out of cylinders of rolled dough.

ENRICHMENTS

- Take a trip to a bakery. Get permission from the bakery first, and then call on the day of the trip to remind them you are coming.
- Examine samples of rice flour, potato flour, rye, oats, cracked wheat, flaxseed, and the like. These may be purchased in a health-food store but not used interchangeably with your regular flour because of their inadequate gluten content. They can be substituted for up to ⅓ the wheat flour in any bread recipe, though. Let the children discuss their tastes, textures, appearances, and smells.
- Make a field trip to some ethnic food stores to buy a variety of interesting breads and rolls such as pita, French bread, panetone, Greek sesame rings, pan dulces, Jewish rye, pumpernickel, Italian bread sticks, Kaiser or Vienna rolls, bagels (water, egg, onion, or pumpernickel), raisin-pumpernickel, flat brot, stollen, corn bread, Boston brown bread, English muffins, crumpets—the list is endless.

Corn Bread

*2 cups cornmeal
1 tsp salt
½ tsp baking soda
1½ tsp baking powder
1 tbsp sugar
2 eggs
1½ cups buttermilk
¼ cup oil*

Equipment

*measuring cups
measuring spoons
large bowl
wooden mixing spoon
sifter
spatula for leveling off
    measurements
9″ × 9″ rectangular pan or
    corn-stick pans, greased*

Yield sixteen 2″ × 2″ pieces

1. Preheat oven to 400°. ☮
2. Sift cornmeal, salt, soda, baking powder, and sugar into a mixing bowl.
3. Stir in unbeaten eggs, buttermilk, and oil, stirring only until all ingredients are mixed.
4. Pour into greased baking pans.
5. Bake 30 minutes, or until lightly browned.

VARIATIONS

- Add 2 mashed, ripe bananas at the end of Step 3. Bake as usual.
- Heat a griddle, and use the batter for pancakes. Grease the griddle well, drop tablespoons of corn bread batter on it, and spread them flat with a spatula. When brown on underside, turn pancakes, and cook on second side until brown. Transfer to a heated plate, and serve with syrup or jam. This makes 24 dollar-size or eight 4-inch pancakes.
- Add ¼ cup bacon bits at the end of Step 3. Bake as usual.
- Top corn bread with maple syrup.
- *Spoon Bread.* Use ½ cup cornmeal or hominy grits, ½ tsp salt, 2 cups milk, 3 eggs, and 1 tbsp margarine. Put cornmeal and salt in a saucepan. Stir in the milk. Cook over direct heat about 5 minutes until thick mush is formed. Remove from heat. Stir in margarine until it melts. Cool. Then add slightly beaten eggs. Turn into buttered casserole. Bake at 375° for 35 or 40 minutes, until the top is puffed and brown. Serve hot from the baking dish with a spoon. May be eaten with butter and/or syrup.
- Add ½ cup corn kernels to batter before baking corn bread or spoon bread.

ENRICHMENTS

- Buy fresh or frozen ears of corn. Taste them raw. Cook 5 minutes in boiling water, spread with butter and salt, and taste again.

- Scrape the kernels from raw ears of corn with a sharp knife. Cook in boiling water until tender (about 5 minutes). Season with butter, salt, and pepper.
- Plant some of the raw kernels (follow directions for planting peas, p. 62).
- Buy canned regular whole-kernel or creamed corn, frozen corn, and fresh corn, and compare the flavors.
- See p. 132 for popcorn recipes.
- Grind raw kernels of corn in a blender, a wheat or coffee grinder, or a metate (Mexican hand stone grinder). Allow the children to work with it and taste it. The ground corn can be used in the recipe for corn bread above.
- Buy canned hominy, drain, add salt and butter, and heat. Serve as a vegetable.
- Buy hominy grits. Prepare according to directions on the package, and serve as a cereal with butter and milk or as a vegetable.
- Buy some of the candy corn that is so popular around Halloween.

Soft Pretzels

1 package dry yeast
¾ cup warm water
1 tsp salt
1 tbsp sugar
2 cups sifted flour
coarse salt (kosher salt)
2 tbsp milk or water

Equipment

large bowl
mixing spoon
wooden breadboard
pastry brush or paintbrush
measuring spoons
measuring cups
spatula
sifter
cookie sheet, greased
cooling rack
wax paper

Yield 12 pretzels 6″ in diameter

1. Preheat oven to 425°.
2. Dissolve yeast in warm water in a large bowl. Be sure water feels comfortably warm to the inner wrist. If the water is too hot, the yeast will die.
3. Add salt and sugar, and mix well.
4. Beat in flour, and knead dough in the bowl until smooth. This may take about 10 minutes. Allow the children to take turns kneading.
5. Turn dough out on a floured board.
6. Have each child pinch off a section of dough 2 inches in diameter and roll it into a rope. This is done most easily by placing both palms on the dough and rolling back and forth on the lightly floured board until the rope is about 12 inches long.
7. Form into a pretzel by shaping the rope into a circle, grasping the two ends, and twisting them around each other several times. Then bring the twisted ends across through the center of the circle to press the ends into the point opposite on the rim, thus forming two halves divided by the twisted ends, as illustrated.

8. Place on a greased baking sheet. Brush surfaces with milk or water, using a pastry brush or a clean paintbrush. Sprinkle liberally with coarse salt.
9. Bake immediately 12 to 15 minutes until nicely browned.
10. Remove from baking sheet, and cool on a rack.

VARIATIONS

- Shape away! Let the children invent their own shapes—letters, numbers, names, flowers, geometric shapes, stylized human figures, and more.
- Use poppy seeds, sesame seeds, chocolate sprinkles, cinnamon sugar, jam glaze, or anything else instead of coarse salt.
- For a softer pretzel, allow the unbaked, shaped forms to rise 15 minutes *covered with a damp towel* to keep them from drying out. Brush with milk, and sprinkle with coarse salt.

ENRICHMENTS

- Buy store pretzels, and compare them to the ones you've made—taste, color, texture, size, and shape.
- Using illustrations, discuss the planting and growth of wheat as one of our most important staple foods.
- Buy a selection of wheat cereals, boil them, and allow the children to taste them. Compare the textures, colors, smells, and flavors.
- Buy a selection of flours such as white, whole-wheat, rye, graham (wheat), rice, soy, and cornmeal. Let the children touch, taste, smell, sift, and mix the flours, as you compare them.
- Buy a variety of cereal grains, such as whole-wheat kernels, oats, rye, barley, rice, millet, corn, and any others you can find. Compare them. If not heat-treated, they can be planted (without soil as directed below) and their growth and development observed. The sprouted grains can be used in sandwiches in place of lettuce or in salads.

Soak seeds in water (to cover) overnight. Drain. Sprinkle soaked seeds on a hand towel that has been dipped in water and wrung out. Place a row of seeds every 4 inches. Fold the towel over the rows of seeds, and water lightly every day to keep moist. After five days, the sprouts may be picked off the unfolded towel for eating or cooking. (For more suggestions for gardens, see p. 64.)

Popping Popovers

2 years–kindergarten
Baking time: 45 minutes

1 cup sifted flour
¼ tsp salt
2 eggs
1 cup milk

Equipment
large bowl
measuring cups
measuring spoons
eggbeater
spatula
wooden spoon

(list continued next page)

1. Preheat oven to 400°. ☬
2. Preheat pans in the oven 5 minutes. ☬
3. Mix unbeaten eggs and milk in the bowl.
4. Sift flour, measure it, and resift with salt.
5. Lightly sift flour-salt mixture into milk-egg mixture.
6. Beat with an eggbeater until mixture is free of lumps.
7. Fill cups or muffin tins ½ to ⅔ full.
8. Place pans in oven (put custard cups on a baking sheet). ☬
9. Bake 30 minutes at 400°, and then reduce to 350° for 10 to 15 minutes longer, depending on the size.
10. Make a small slit in the top of each popover with a paring knife to allow steam to escape.
11. Remove from pans, and serve while still hot, with butter and jam.

Yield 8 to 12 popovers

VARIATIONS

- *Nut Popovers.* Additional ingredients are 1 or 2 tbsp finely chopped nuts (almonds, peanuts, walnuts, pecans, or pistachio nuts). Sprinkle nuts on tops of unbaked popovers. Bake as usual.
- *Bacon Popovers.* Additional ingredients are 2 tbsp imitation bacon bits or 3 strips of bacon. Fry bacon until crisp, and drain on paper towels. Sprinkle finely crumbled bacon or bits on tops, and bake as usual.
- *Parsley Popovers.* Blend 1 tbsp dried parsley flakes or 2 tbsp chopped fresh parsley into egg mixture in Step 6, and bake as usual.
- *Chili Popovers.* Blend 2 tsp chili powder into egg mixture, and bake as usual.
- *Cheese Popovers.* Blend ¼ cup grated Parmesan or grated American cheese into egg mixture, and bake as usual.
- Try blending in other spices or seasonings, such as 1 tsp dried sweet basil, 1 tsp ground cardamom, 1 tsp cinnamon, 1 tsp marjoram, or ½ tsp nutmeg.
- The hollow cavity formed inside a popover as it bakes is a natural container for other foods. When done, you can cut off the tops and fill the bottoms right away with such surprises as scrambled eggs, jam or jelly, cottage cheese, chive cottage cheese, cooked hamburger, chili with beans, creamed chicken, shrimp or tuna salad, creamed shrimp or tuna, or beef stew. Replace tops, and serve.

ENRICHMENTS

- Discuss how the hole in the center of a popover occurs. (Popovers have a large proportion of eggs and liquid and are baked at a rather high temperature, which generates steam, causing extremely rapid expansion of the batter as it bakes, thus producing the hole in the middle.
- Compare popovers to biscuits, muffins, toast, regular bread, cake, and cupcakes, and discuss taste, texture, and appearance.

Baking-Powder Biscuits

2 cups sifted flour
1 tsp salt
2 tsp sugar
4 tsp baking powder
¼ cup margarine
⅔ cup milk

Equipment
sifter
measuring spoons
measuring cups
mixing bowl
spatula
wax paper
2 table knives or a pastry
*   blender*
fork
breadboard or pastry board
baking sheet

Yield 12 to 15 biscuits

1. Preheat oven to 425°.
2. Sift flour, measure it, and then resift with salt, sugar, and baking powder into a bowl.
3. Cut the margarine into the flour with two knives in a crisscross cutting motion until the pieces of margarine are the size of coarse cornmeal. If you prefer, margarine can be rubbed into the flour between thumb and forefinger, instead.
4. Pour milk quickly into the flour mixture, stir with a fork by pushing the fork into the dough mixture and bringing it up through the dough. This helps keep dough aerated and light so the biscuits won't be heavy. If all the flour is not incorporated in the mass, add a tablespoon or more of milk. The dough should be light and soft but not sticky.
5. Turn the dough onto a lightly floured board.
6. Lightly knead the dough about 20 seconds. Do not overknead.
7. Pat or lightly roll the dough to ½-inch thickness. Cut with a round biscuit cutter dipped in flour.
8. Place the biscuits on a baking sheet about ½ inch apart. (Greasing the sheet is not necessary.)
9. Use up the scraps by forming them into a ball, rerolling, and cutting out more rounds.
10. Bake 12 to 15 minutes.

VARIATIONS

- *Cheese Biscuits.* Add ½ cup grated American or Swiss cheese to flour-margarine mixture.
- *Orange Biscuits.* Before baking, press a lump of sugar that has been dipped into orange juice into each biscuit, and sprinkle with a pinch of grated orange rind.
- *Cinnamon Pinwheels* or *Butterscotch Sticky Buns.* Roll dough into a rectangle ½ inch thick, spread with softened margarine, and sprinkle with ½ cup sugar mixed with 2 tsp cinnamon

for cinnamon pinwheels. Sprinkle with ½ cup brown sugar for butterscotch buns. You may add nuts, raisins, or coconut to either. Roll into a cylindrical tube as for a jelly roll. Cut with a sharp knife into 1-inch slices. Place cut side down on a greased baking pan. Bake at 400° for 15 to 20 minutes.

- *Drop Biscuits.* Increase milk to 1 cup, so batter will drop from a spoon onto a greased baking sheet. Bake 12 to 15 minutes.

ENRICHMENTS

(See p. 114.)

Toast

2 years–kindergarten
Toasting time: around 5 minutes

a variety of breads (whole-wheat, raisin, white, rye, pumpernickel, oatmeal, as well as muffins, biscuits, rolls, and such), with spare pieces for seconds and for burning
spreads such as butter, jam, honey, brown sugar, regular sugar, grated American cheese, peanut butter, cinnamon, cream cheese, orange marmalade, jelly, garlic butter, orange juice, and orange rind

Equipment
electric toaster or broiler
cookie sheet (if you use a broiler)
table knives
plates
spoons for spreads

(Although this may seem unnecessarily simple, many children have not had the opportunity to make toast. Variety is important here, too, so they don't feel they always have to have routine pieces of white-bread toast.)

1. Set the broiler at 500°, or use a toaster if you have one.
2. For the broiler, arrange bread on a cookie sheet, and then place it on a broiling rack about 2 inches below the heat source.
3. Brown on one side.
4. Turn, and brown on the other side.

Remove to plates while still warm, and spread with softened butter and a spread or one of the following variations.

VARIATIONS

- *Cinnamon Toast.* Mix ½ cup sugar and 2 tsp cinnamon. Sprinkle on buttered toast.
- *Butterscotch Toast.* Sprinkle buttered toast with brown sugar.
- *Orange Toast.* ½ cup sugar, 1 tbsp orange juice and 1 tsp grated orange rind, well mixed.
- Have several varieties of honey for tasting.
- Beat ½ cup peanut butter, ¼ cup honey, and ½ cube softened butter together. Spread on toast.
- Add ½ cup grated American cheese, and return toast to broiler only long enough to melt the cheese. Sprinkle with garlic salt, if you like.
- Cream cheese and jam make a good combination by spreading each on half the toast and folding to make a sandwich. Any variety of jelly or jam may be used, but grape is a particular favorite.
- *Milk Toast.* Place buttered toast in a shallow bowl, and pour ½ cup hot milk over it. Voilà—milk toast! Sprinkle with sugar, if desired.

- *Melba Toast.* Set oven at 250°. Cut bread in ⅛-inch-thick slices, and place on cookie sheet. Bake 1 hour, until bread is dry and an even golden color. Spread with softened butter. The bread may be cut into a variety of shapes before baking, so you can discuss shapes at the table. Try sticks, circles, cookie-cutter shapes, rings (using a doughnut cutter), triangles, squares, matchsticks (as fine as possible). Cut into ¼-inch squares for "croutons," and sprinkle them in a salad or on soup. Children may also enjoy eating them plain.
- *Toast Cups.* Trim crusts from thinly sliced bread, and roll them lightly with a rolling pin. Spread both sides with softened butter. Press each slice down into a hole of a small muffin pan so that the bread forms a cup with four triangular sides. Bake in a 350° oven about 20 minutes, or until cups are crisp and brown. Fill with any filling, and serve.

ENRICHMENTS

- Cut toast into squares, halves, or fingers, and discuss shapes and fractions.
- Have a variety of honey in such flavors as orange, sage, clover, and buckwheat, and in such forms as creamed, comb, or fluid.
- Weigh bread before and after toasting. Point out that toasted bread is lighter because it loses water during cooking.
- Return toast to toaster or oven, and show the children the stages of darkening. Purposefully burn a slice to illustrate the cooking process carried to the ultimate. Let the brave ones taste all stages! Discuss smell and taste. ☝
- Purchase a variety of breads (like those listed at beginning of this recipe), and have a tasting party. Discuss grain, texture, appearance, color, smell, and taste. Freeze unused bread to use later.
- There is a special kitchen gadget that will cut a single slice of bread in half crosswise to make a very thin slice. This is interesting to observe and discuss.
- A variety of cheeses may be used on the toast. Discuss taste, texture, smell, color.
- A variety of jams or jellies may open a discussion of fruit, its sources, flavors, textures, smells, and so on.

French Toast

1 egg
½ cup milk
⅛ tsp salt
1 tbsp sugar
½ tsp vanilla extract
4 slices bread
oil for skillet

Equipment

griddle or skillet
measuring cups
measuring spoons
bowl
eggbeater
fork or broad pancake
*   turner*
pie plate or other shallow
*   dish*

Yield 4 slices French toast

1. Preheat griddle or skillet to 375°, and grease it lightly. ↻
2. Beat egg in a bowl until it is well blended.
3. Add milk, salt, sugar, and vanilla to the egg.
4. Pour into a pie plate or other shallow dish.
5. Dip each piece of bread into the milk-egg mixture, front and back, until well soaked.
6. Lift bread with a fork or a broad pancake turner, letting excess liquid drain back into the dish.
7. Brown on both sides in griddle or skillet (takes about 5 minutes). Add fat if needed.
8. Transfer to warmed plate, butter, sprinkle with powdered sugar or cinnamon sugar.

VARIATIONS

- Omit sugar, and serve with maple or other pancake syrup.
- Serve with jam or jelly.
- Use different kinds of bread, such as raisin, egg, whole-wheat, oatmeal, or French, and discuss the differences.
- Add ½ tsp of any other flavoring, such as orange or lemon, to milk-egg mixture.
- Substitute orange juice for half the milk, and add another tsp sugar. Or try other juices, such as pineapple, apricot, peach nectar, apple, and prune.
- Instead of frying, place 4 slices of bread in a shallow baking pan, and pour milk-egg mixture over it. Bake at least 30 minutes at 350°, or until brown. Use toppings as desired. The French call this *pain perdu*, meaning "lost bread," and use up their leftover bread in this delicious way.

ENRICHMENTS

- Discuss the manufacture of bread, and see Bread Sculptures, p. 130.
- Visit a bakery.

- Go to the market as a class. Let the children choose a variety of breads to buy. Leftovers can be frozen. Compare appearances, tastes, and textures.
- Plant some wheat (see p. 119).
- Grind whole-kernel wheat in a blender or food grinder. Cook in boiling, salted water about 10 minutes. (Measure twice as much water as ground wheat.) Serve as a cereal. One cup uncooked makes 4 servings cooked.

Pancakes

2 cups flour
2 eggs, beaten
2 cups milk
2 tsp baking powder
½ cup shortening, melted
1 tbsp sugar
1 tsp salt
powdered sugar, flavored
  syrups, jam, jelly, or
  pureed fruit (p. 59)

Equipment

meauring spoons
measuring cups
large bowl
small bowl
mixing spoon
pancake turner
griddle, heavy skillet, or
  electric griddle, greased
flour sifter
eggbeater
spatula
wax paper

Yield 32 dollar-size pancakes

1. Preheat griddle or skillet to 375°.
2. Sift and measure flour into the large mixing bowl.
3. Measure baking powder, salt, and sugar, and add them to the flour.
4. Sift all dry ingredients together.
5. Break eggs into the small bowl. Add milk and melted shortening. Mix well.
6. Make a well in the dry ingredients.
7. Add liquid ingredients to the dry ingredients all at once. Mix thoroughly, but do not over-mix. Mixture will be lumpy.
8. Test preheated griddle with a drop of water (water should dance if it is hot enough). It is not necessary to grease the griddle.
9. Drop batter onto griddle by tablespoonfuls. Cook until bubbles appear.
10. Turn over with a pancake turner.
11. Continue cooking until pancakes are brown on the second side.
12. Remove to plates, and sprinkle with powdered sugar or any other topping.

Children may eat these with their fingers as soon as they are cool enough to handle. This method makes dollar-size pancakes. (They can also be made larger.)

VARIATIONS

- Pancake mix can be used, by following the directions on the package.
- Substitute 1 tsp soda and 2½ cups buttermilk for baking powder and milk to make buttermilk pancakes.
- Slices of fruit, such as apples, peaches, pears, or bananas (fresh or canned) may be added to individual pancakes (1 tbsp each) as soon as each one is spooned onto the griddle. Turn them with a wide pancake turner.

- Toppings for the cooked pancakes can be varied. Use butter, cinnamon and sugar, brown or colored white sugar, syrup (maple, corn, fruit), honey, nuts, coconut.
- Make pancake animals or cookies by placing open, metal cookie cutters on the griddle and spooning batter in their open spaces. (Brush the cookie cutters with oil inside and out before using.) Do *not* use plastic cookie cutters, as they may melt. Leave the cutters on while the pancakes cook.
- Spread one pancake with filling such as peanut butter, jam, cooked strips of bacon, or cooked ham or sausage, and cover with a second pancake.
- Pancake batter can be made by placing all ingredients in a blender container at one time. Be sure to cut the recipe in half, or the blender container will be too full. Mix until moistened, and proceed in the same way.

ENRICHMENTS

- Use this lesson as a starting point for telling the interesting story of making maple syrup, using pictures to illustrate the discussion so it will be clearer for the children.
- Point out how the pancakes rise as they cook. Explain that this is because of the release of carbon dioxide by the baking powder or baking soda when moistened and heated.
- This lesson may be the basis for an illustrated lecture on how sugar is made and how it is possible for us to have so many kinds of sugar.

Energy Crunch

1 cup rolled oats (uncooked)
1 cup wheat germ
1 cup sesame seeds
1 cup coconut (flaked or
*   shredded)*
⅓ cup vegetable oil
½ cup honey or brown sugar

Equipment

measuring cups
bowl
mixing spoon
baking pan or cookie sheet
spatula

Yield 4 cups breakfast cereal
    or topping

1. Preheat oven to 325°. ☝
2. Mix oats, wheat germ, sesame seeds, coconut, and oil in a bowl.
3. Gradually blend in honey or sugar.
4. Spread on baking pan or cookie sheet.
5. Bake 30 minutes, stirring occasionally.
6. Remove from oven, and cool.

Break into small pieces, and serve as snacks or as a cereal with milk.

VARIATIONS

- Add ½ cup any kind of chopped nuts before baking. Whole Spanish peanuts are especially good.
- After baking, add ½ cup to 1 cup of any chopped, dried fruit. Be sure to mix well.
- If used as a cereal, garnish with fresh or canned fruit.
- To serve as dessert, crumble into a dish, and cover with canned fruit and juice.
- Crumble over ice-cream, to add nutritional value.

ENRICHMENTS

- Compare the various forms of oatmeal—regular, long-cooking, quick-cooking, and instant.
- Sow some oats! Let the children plant some whole-kernel oats in their garden (see p. 119).
- Toast some sesame seeds by spreading them in a pan in a 350° oven about 10 minutes, or until lightly browned. Stir occasionally. Let the children compare them with the raw sesame seeds.
- Make Tahini, a Mediterranean food of many uses, which is raw sesame seeds ground to a smooth, creamy consistency in the blender. Have the children taste, and then add honey to sweeten. Use as a supernutritious snack by spreading it on graham crackers or toast.
- Review enrichments on wheat (pp. 114, 118, 126).

Bread Masks and Sculptures

4 years–kindergarten
Baking time: 10–15 minutes

2 cups flour
3 tbsp oil
½ cup to 1 cup lukewarm
  water
½ tsp salt

Equipment
measuring cups
measuring spoons
wooden mixing spoon
large bowl
breadboard
spatula
wax paper
pie tins or tart tins (1 for
  each child who is cooking)
cooling rack

Yield 6 large masks, more
  tart-size masks

1. Preheat oven to 350°. ☂
2. Sift flour, and then measure it into a bowl. Add salt.
3. Add oil, and rub it into the flour and salt with your fingertips until the mixture resembles coarse cornmeal.
4. Make a well in the center of the mixture, and pour about ½ cup water into it. Blend with fingertips or a spoon. Pour in remaining water, a tablespoon at a time, as needed to form a dough that can be gathered into a ball.
5. Knead the dough in the bowl by pushing back on it with the heel of your hand, turning the dough over, and pulling it forward. Children love to help with this. If the dough is too sticky, add a little flour. It takes at least 10 minutes of kneading for the dough to become smooth and elastic.
6. Cover the dough with a damp cloth, and let it rest at least 15 minutes.
7. Divide the dough into 6 equal balls. Roll each ball out on a lightly floured board until it is 8 inches in diameter.
8. Place on the flat part of an upside-down pie or tart tin. Trim off excess dough with scissors. Cut through the dough with a small, sharp knife, to cut out facial features.
9. Place dough-covered pie tins on cookie sheets.
10. Bake at 350° for 10 to 15 minutes, or until lightly browned.
11. Cool on a rack. Remove from pie tins.
12. Paint with diluted food color as desired.

VARIATIONS

• Should a child wish to preserve the bread mask, place the painted mask in a 250° oven about 8 hours, to dry out completely. Then paint or spray it with clear lacquer or shellac. If the mask is to be hung, make an additional hole in the top before baking, or glue a picture hook on the inside of the mask.

- *Glove Sculptures.* Use a child's hand as a pattern. Hold the hand on the dough with a slight pressure, and cut around it with a sharp knife. Another way to do this that involves more sensory experience is to paint the child's hand with tempera or any other washable paint and then have the child press down on the rolled-out dough. Use the paint print to cut out the glove sculpture. Bake as for bread masks. If a tracing wheel is available, that will also work in cutting out the dough. The uncolored hands can be painted after baking, with the details of the hand. The glove sculptures can also be decorated in the unbaked stage by attaching rolled-out pieces of dough cut into the shapes of flowers, initials, or other designs. Moisten the pieces of dough slightly with a finger dipped in water, and press them gently onto the glove.
- You can purchase frozen prepared bread dough instead, thaw it, and use it as above. Refrigerator biscuits can also be used, by pressing two or three together, rolling them out, and proceeding in the same way.
- If there is not enough time to make the dough and bake it the same day, the dough may be covered with a damp cloth and refrigerated until the next day, when it can be used as above.

Pop Goes the Popcorn

*8 ounces colored popping
  corn*
oil to cover bottom of pan
salt (optional)
melted butter (optional)

Equipment
electric skillet
*1 clean double-bed sheet (to
  catch popped corn)*
serving bowls
paper cups or plates

Yield enough for the class,
  with extra to share or take
  home

1. Spread the sheet on the floor in the work area.
2. Connect the skillet to an outlet, and place it in the center of the sheet, pushing the sheet close to the skillet, so no one walks on it.
3. Pour oil into the skillet to about ⅛-inch depth.
4. Heat to 450°, until oil starts to smoke.
5. Teacher should pour unpopped corn carefully into the heated skillet.
6. Have all the children spread out the edges of the sheet and raise them to shoulder height.
7. Allow corn to pop. Popped corn will fly in all directions from the pan, to be caught in the bedsheet. (When corn starts popping, unplug the skillet.)
8. Collect popped corn in a serving bowl, and take it to the table. Salt, and pour melted butter on it, if you like.
9. Let children help themselves from the bowl. Let them place their own servings of popcorn on paper plates or in paper cups.

VARIATIONS

- Popcorn balls can be made from the popped corn (before salting or adding butter). Be sure to remove unpopped corn first. Then pour candy syrup (see below) over popped corn in a bowl. When cool enough to handle, shape popcorn with buttered hands. Set the balls on cookie sheets covered with wax paper for ½ hour to cool and harden. Children can make balls of graduated sizes, which when put together before hardening will make Santa Clauses, snowmen, or any other figures. The figures can be decorated with raisins or chocolate chips or pieces of maraschino cherries. They can be dressed with paper hats and ribbons or other such materials.

- *Syrup for Popcorn Balls*. Put 1 cup molasses, 1 cup corn syrup, and 1 tbsp distilled vinegar into a large saucepan. Boil, stirring constantly, until the thermometer reaches the soft-crack stage (when it hardens so it can be broken easily after being dropped into cold water), or 270° on a candy thermometer. This makes enough for 8 cups of popcorn.
- Commercial marshmallow syrup can be warmed slightly and used instead of homemade syrup for popcorn balls.
- Puffed rice or puffed wheat can be substituted for the popcorn in making the balls.
- Popcorn or puffed cereals with either homemade syrup or marshmallow syrup may be poured into a pan and allowed to harden. The sweet can then be cut into squares and eaten as a snack or dessert or else taken home to share. A wooden lollipop stick can be pushed into each piece to make popcorn lollipops, or "poppy-lops."

ENRICHMENTS

- Set aside some popped and unpopped corn. Children can make free-form mosaics by gluing them on paper. This can be a creative project to take home.
- Compare fresh or frozen ears of corn with unpopped corn, popped corn. Indian corn, hominy, cornmeal, and corn bread. Discuss the differences in color, odor, texture, volume, and flavor. Allow children to look, touch, and taste as much as possible.
- Buy an ear of corn with the husk and corn silk still on. Explain how corn grows. Show some pictures of cornfields.
- Plant some corn kernels, and watch them grow (p. 62).

Basic Plain Cake

2 years–kindergarten
Baking time: cake, 30–35 minutes;
cupcakes, 15–20 minutes

¼ cup softened butter or
   margarine
1 cup sugar
1 egg
2 cups sifted cake flour
2½ tsp baking powder
½ tsp salt
¾ cup milk
1 tsp vanilla extract

Equipment

large bowl
mixing spoon
measuring spoons
measuring cups
spatula
sifter
wax paper

1. Preheat oven to 350°. ☂
2. Sift flour onto wax paper. Measure.
3. Return flour to sifter, add baking powder and salt, and sift together three times, to mix well.
4. Place butter in a large bowl, cream well by beating against the side of the bowl with a spoon until light and pliable.
5. Gradually add sugar, and continue beating until well blended.
6. Beat egg in a small bowl till well blended, and add it to the butter-sugar mixture, mixing it in well.
7. Add vanilla to the milk.
8. Gradually add the flour mixture and the milk-vanilla mixture alternately to the butter-sugar-egg mixture.
9. Mix all ingredients. Pour into two greased and floured round cake pans (8 or 9 inches in diameter) or 12 cupcake wells (to ⅔ full) or one 9-inch square pan.
10. Bake cake 30 to 35 minutes. Bake cupcakes 15 to 20 minutes. Cupcake pans may have paper cupcake liners, to facilitate cleaning and serving. Aluminum-foil cupcake forms can be set directly on a cookie sheet.

*baking pans (two 8'' or 9''
    diameter or one 9'' × 9'')
    or a 12-well muffin tin,
    greased and floured*
small bowl
cooling rack

Yield two 8-inch or 9-inch cake
layers or 12 cupcakes

11. Test for doneness by checking any of the following points: cake is evenly browned, it springs back immediately when pressed lightly in the center with a finger, it pulls away from the side of the pan, and a toothpick or knife inserted in the center comes out clean. Beware of overbaking.
12. Cool right side up on a raised rack about 5 minutes; then remove from pan, and allow to finish cooling on rack.

VARIATIONS

- A quick method is to start with the softened butter, add the flour mixture and the remaining ingredients, and beat vigorously until smooth. (An electric beater may be used.) Cake will not be as fine-grained.
- *Chocolate Cake.* Add 2 ounces cooled, melted chocolate or 1 cup melted chocolate chips before adding the flour, or ½ cup cocoa sifted with the dry ingredients. Reduce flour by ½ cup when using cocoa.
- *Fruit-Flavored Cake.* After Step 8 add ½ cup chopped fruit (canned, fresh, or frozen) such as peaches, apricots, cherries, apples, pineapples, or bananas. Drain first.
- *Nut Cake.* Add 1 cup coconut or chopped nuts of any variety after Step 8.
- *Marble Cake.* Divide batter in half, add 1 ounce cooled, melted chocolate to one half, and mix well. Place alternate spoonfuls of chocolate and plain batter in pans. When complete, draw a table knife through the batter in any direction two or three times, to make a more interesting design.
- Use a variety of icings and frostings on the cupcakes.
- Use different food colorings in the batter and the frostings.
- Fill cupcake wells ½ full. Bury a surprise in each, such as a miniature marshmallow, a jelly bean, a gumdrop, a chocolate chip, a maraschino cherry, a spoonful of peanut butter, or any other edible delicacy. Cover with remaining batter to ⅔ full, and bake as before.

Puddle Cake

1½ cups sifted flour
1 cup sugar
3 tbsp cocoa
1 tsp baking soda
½ tsp salt
6 tbsp oil
1 tbsp vinegar
1 tsp vanilla extract
1 cup water

Equipment
baking pan (9-inch square
* or round), lightly greased*
fork
measuring spoons
measuring cups
sifter
spatula
wax paper
cooling rack

Yield one 9-inch cake

1. Preheat oven to 350°.
2. Place dry ingredients directly in lightly greased baking pan.
3. Make three indentations in this mixture with the back of a measuring tablespoon. Place oil in one, vinegar in the second, and vanilla extract in the third. Drizzle water over all. Mix well with the fork. Now it looks like *mud pies*.
4. Bake 25 minutes.
5. Cool about 5 minutes in the pan. Remove from pan, and continue cooling on a rack.
6. Frost as desired.

Experimental Cake

flour
baking powder
sugar
eggs
milk
oil
salt
margarine
chocolate chips
raisins
peanuts or other nuts
vanilla extract

Equipment
bowls
measuring cups
measuring spoons
sifter
spatula
mixing spoons
various baking pans,
   greased
wax paper
cooling rack

For extra fun, have individual children or the group make their very own cakes, by having all the following ingredients available and letting them combine them as they wish. This is for children who have had some experience in baking. Teachers should guide but not lead. Even a failure is a valid experience.

1. Preheat oven to 350°. ☻
2. Put all ingredients on the table. ☻
3. Let each child choose something to add, *the children tasting the mixture to correct the flavor as they proceed.*
4. When the children are through, pour the batter into a greased baking pan.
5. Bake until done. (Start testing with a straw or a knife after 30 minutes.)

This can be a most unusual experience for children who are interested and experienced in cooking. It is best done with older children who have some awareness of what is being attempted.

VARIATIONS

- *Cake Candles.* Fill greased juice cans ⅔ full with cake batter, and bake at 350° for 15 to 20 minutes (or until done). Allow to cool until it is easy to open the bottom ends with a can opener and push the metal pieces through, forcing the cakes out. Cool completely, and ice as desired. Place a birthday candle in the top of each, arrange any number of cakes you like (or one for each child), and use them instead of a traditional birthday cake. The average cake mix or batter with 2 cups flour will make 8 cake candles.
- Cut out a large paper pattern of an animal, a geometric shape, a flower, a heart, or whatever. Place one on the top of a cake, and cut around the pattern with a sharp knife to make an unusual shaped cake.

- Place a lacy paper doily or cookie cutters on top of the cake, and dust with powdered sugar to make interesting shapes. Remove paper or cutters, being careful not to let surplus powdered sugar drop back onto the cake. A variation is to let the older children cut out their own lacy doilies from folded paper.

ENRICHMENTS

- Discuss how baking powder and baking soda make a cake rise and change volume when they get wet, decompose, and generate carbon dioxide.
- Point out how different pans make cakes of different shapes. Try using pans of unusual shape.
- Be sure to purchase a cake to compare with the cake(s) the class makes.

Goldilocks's Brownies

2 years–kindergarten
Baking time: 30 minutes

½ *cup margarine*
2 ounces or 2 squares
  unsweetened baking
  chocolate
½ *tsp salt*
1 cup sugar
2 eggs
1 tsp vanilla extract
½ *cup chopped nuts*
  (optional)
¾ *cup flour*
½ *tsp baking powder*

1. Preheat oven to 325°.
2. Melt margarine and chocolate in saucepan over *low* heat.
3. Cool, and transfer to a mixing bowl.
4. Mix in sugar, salt, eggs (one at a time), vanilla, nuts, flour, and baking powder.
5. Pour batter into the greased pan, and spread evenly.
6. Bake about 30 minutes.
7. Cool slightly, and cut into squares.

VARIATIONS

- *Butterscotch Brownies*. Omit chocolate, and substitute 1 cup brown sugar for the white sugar. For added flavor, add ½ cup butterscotch bits, either as they come out of the package or melted.

Equipment

measuring cups
measuring spoons
sifter
spatula
mixing spoon
small saucepan
bowl
8″ × 8″ baking pan, greased
wax paper

Yield 16 or more brownies

• *Coconut Brownies.* Add ½ cup shredded coconut.
• *Spice Brownies.* Add 1 tsp cinnamon, ½ tsp nutmeg, and ½ tsp powdered ginger.
• *Simple Frosting.* Cream ¼ cup margarine, add 2 tsp cocoa, 2 cups sifted powdered sugar, 2 tbsp cream or milk, and 1 tsp vanilla extract. Beat until smooth. Spread on brownies when they are cool.
• *Peanut-Butter Frosting.* When brownies are still warm, frost the tops with peanut butter (smooth or crunchy).

ENRICHMENTS

• Brownies contain very little baking powder, so they do not rise as high as regular cake. Some of the children may remember the difference in texture between a cake and the brownies. You might freeze a sample for comparison with another cake at a later date.
• Buy chocolate in many forms, such as cocoa, baking chocolate in squares, semisweet chocolate in squares, chocolate bits, and melted chocolate in individual packages. Compare textures, flavors, appearances, and colors.
• *Make Hot Cocoa.* Put 2 tbsp sugar, 4 tbsp cocoa, and ⅛ tsp salt in a saucepan. Stir over low heat in ½ cup water, to form a smooth paste. Stir in 4 cups milk, and continue stirring until hot. Remove from heat to add 1 tsp vanilla. May be topped with whipped cream and cinnamon. This will yield eight ½-cup servings.
• *Make Hot Chocolate.* Substitute 1 ounce (1 square) baking chocolate, melted, for the cocoa, and proceed as in the cocoa recipe above. Explain the difference between cocoa and chocolate to the children (cocoa is made by removing most of the cocoa butter from the chocolate).
• *Make Chocolate Sodas.* For each serving pour soda water over 2 tbsp liquid chocolate mixed with 1 tbsp ice-cream or table cream. Add a scoop of ice-cream on top.

Gingerbread House Pattern

Recipe, p. 142, makes 3 houses this size.

Cut one with a door and one without, saving the cutout door to attach to the front of the house as if it were open.

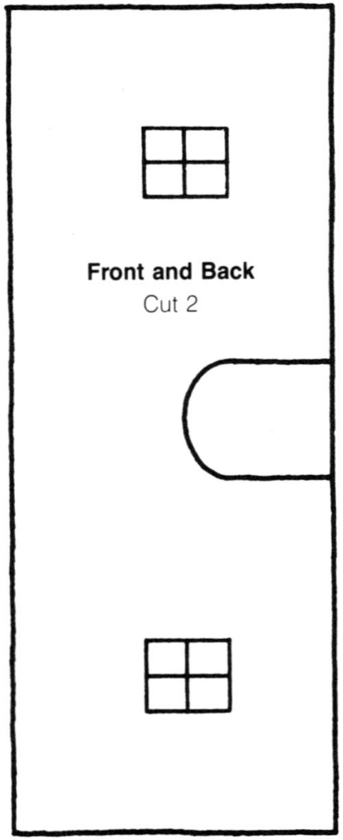

Front and Back
Cut 2

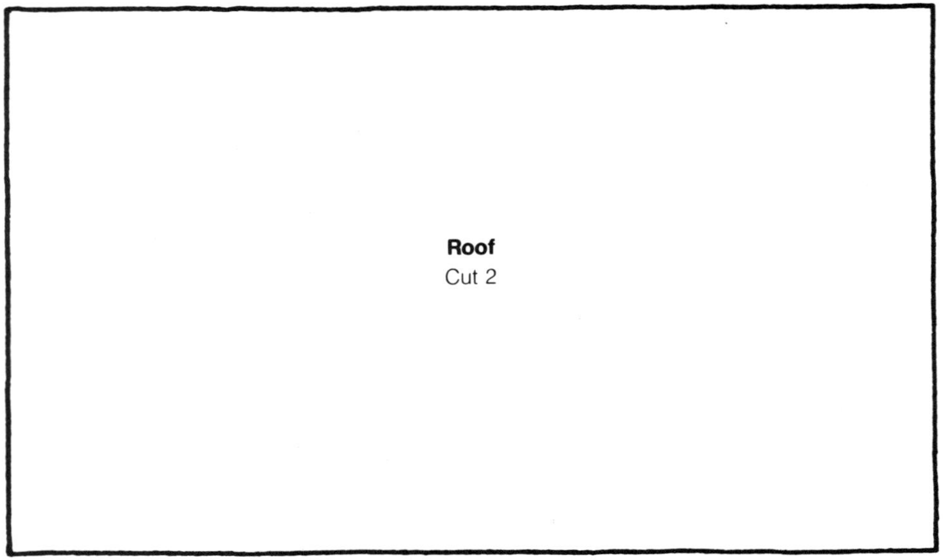

Roof
Cut 2

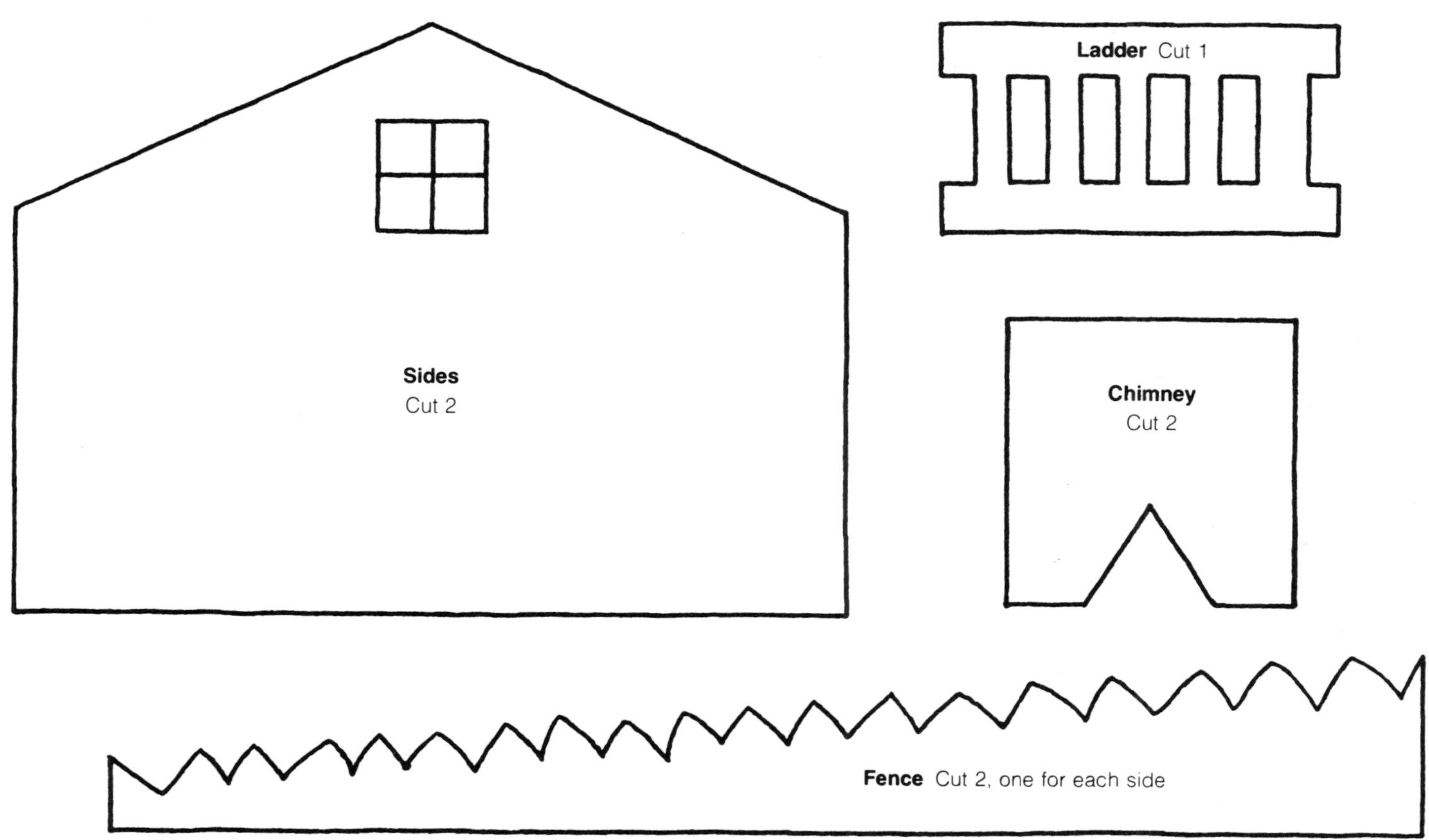

Ladder Cut 1
Sides
Cut 2
Chimney
Cut 2
Fence Cut 2, one for each side

Gingerbread Houses

1 egg
⅓ cup brown sugar
⅔ cup molasses
⅓ cup melted shortening
2¾ cups flour
1 tsp salt
1 pinch soda
1 tsp ginger
2 tsp cinnamon

Equipment

small bowl
large bowl
measuring cups
measuring spoons
spatula
sifter
wax paper
mixing spoon
fork for beating
*jelly-roll pan (about 7″ ×
   11″), greased*
breadboard
cooling rack
pattern (pp. 140–141)
*3 cardboard, wood, or Styro-
   foam bases for houses*

Yield 3 gingerbread houses

1. Preheat oven to 375°. ☻
2. Sift dry ingredients individually onto wax paper, and then measure them into a large bowl.
3. Mix molasses and shortening together in a small bowl.
4. Add that mixture to the dry ingredients.
5. Add the egg, slightly beaten.
6. Mix. Dough should be soft.
7. Roll on a floured breadboard to ¼-inch thickness, and cut out pattern pieces.
8. Bake on a greased pan 10 minutes.
9. Cool on rack.
10. Assemble houses, using frosting for glue, snow, and window panes (apply it with fingers).
11. Decorate the outsides with gumdrops for plants and house decorations. Add candy canes and Christmas candy to the gardens.
12. Glue each house onto a base with frosting.

FROSTING

Beat 4 cups powdered sugar and 2 egg whites together with a mixing spoon until frosting drips slowly enough off a knife to make an icicle. *Do not beat egg whites alone.*

VARIATION

- You may also want inch-thick Styrofoam, wood, or heavy cardboard for bases to rest the houses on; Christmas candy and small candy canes; small "trees"; a Santa Claus head for inside the chimney, or a snowman for the yard from the dime store; powdered sugar for additional snow.

Gingerbread Cookies

⅓ cup margarine
1 cup light brown sugar
1½ cup molasses
⅔ cup water
6 cups sifted flour
2 tsp baking soda
1 tsp salt
1 tsp cinnamon
½ tsp nutmeg
1 tsp ginger

Equipment
bowl
mixing spoons
measuring cups
measuring spoons
spatula
sifter
wax paper
cookie cutters
cookie sheet
breadboard
rolling pin

Yield 24 cookies (halve the recipe for half the yield)

1. Preheat oven to 350°. ☂
2. Cream margarine in a bowl.
3. Add sugar. Mix well.
4. Add molasses, and mix thoroughly.
5. Add water, and mix again.
6. Sift remaining dry ingredients together. Add ⅓ at a time to the other mixture, beating thoroughly after each addition. If dough is sticky, add flour.
7. Roll out on a floured breadboard to ¼-inch thickness. Cut with cookie cutters.
8. Bake on wax paper on a cookie sheet ½ inch apart, about 10 minutes until they are slightly brown (time varies with thickness and size).

VARIATIONS

- Make sculptures of various shapes, using hands, a knife, or clay-modeling tools.
- Make faces, and add raisins, nuts, or cherries for features. Shredded coconut may be added for hair.
- Sprinkle unbaked cookies with a mixture of 1 tsp cinnamon and ¼ cup sugar.
- Make cookie figures using child-designed paper patterns (or cutters), and cut around them with a sharp knife. Bake as usual.
- Cut with a doughnut cutter, and sprinkle with colored sugar. Punch a hole near one edge, so a string can be drawn through it after baking. This can be used as a Christmas tree decoration.
- Cookies can be frosted after baking and cooling, and then sprinkled with colored sugar, brown sugar, coconut, chocolate sprinkles, nonpareils, candy confetti, or nuts (see p. 86).
- Use hands as patterns for the cookies. Place children's hands on the rolled-out dough, and trace around them with a sharp knife. Bake as usual.

- *Punch and Judy Party*. Betsy Brown, creator of the Mr. Hush Puppy Puppet, has originated this clever party idea.

    Our favorite punch is *Punch's Punch* (or else make your own favorite): Dilute 1 can frozen lemonade concentrate as directed. Add 32-ounces pineapple juice, 1 tray ice cubes, and 24-ounces chilled Bubble-Up (a citrus-flavored carbonated drink). Add a few drops of red food coloring if you want pink lemonade. This makes about 3 quarts and keeps well for a week if any is left over.

    For *Betsy Brown's "Judy" Cookies*, roll out basic gingerbread cookie dough as usual. Cut around the edges of a cardboard Judy pattern (traced from the pattern here) to make shaped cookies. Bake as usual. Decorate, if you wish, with commercial tube frosting or home-made frosting, and raisins or nuts. Or paint in features with food coloring.

    You can cut from the same pattern to make Punch and then change the angle of the cookie's nose and chin and pull the topknot into a pointed cap, as shown.

    This theme is especially good for Halloween, open house, children's birthday parties, or visiting adults. (Don't forget to tell the children the story of Punch and Judy.)

- *Colored-Glass Cookies*. Roll out dough into 6-inch ropes ½ inch thick. Join the strips to form the outlines of any open designs—circles, squares, triangles, rectangles, fingers, animal shapes—on a sheet of wax paper placed on a cookie sheet. You can draw the figures on the wax paper first with a blunt pencil, to make the pattern easier to follow. If cookies are to be hung as decorations, make a hole at the top of each with an ice pick. Bake until dough is just beginning to change color (8 to 10 minutes). Remove from oven, and let cool 10 minutes.⊕   While baking, remove sticks from several lollipops of assorted colors, wrap each color separately in a cloth and crush with a hammer on a wooden board or chopping block. (Be careful not to do it on tile or formica, as it may damage the surface.) Colored hard candies can be used instead of lollipops. Put each color of crushed candy in a separate dish. When cookies are cool, fill each of the open spaces in the designs with a thin layer of one color

Judy Cookie Pattern

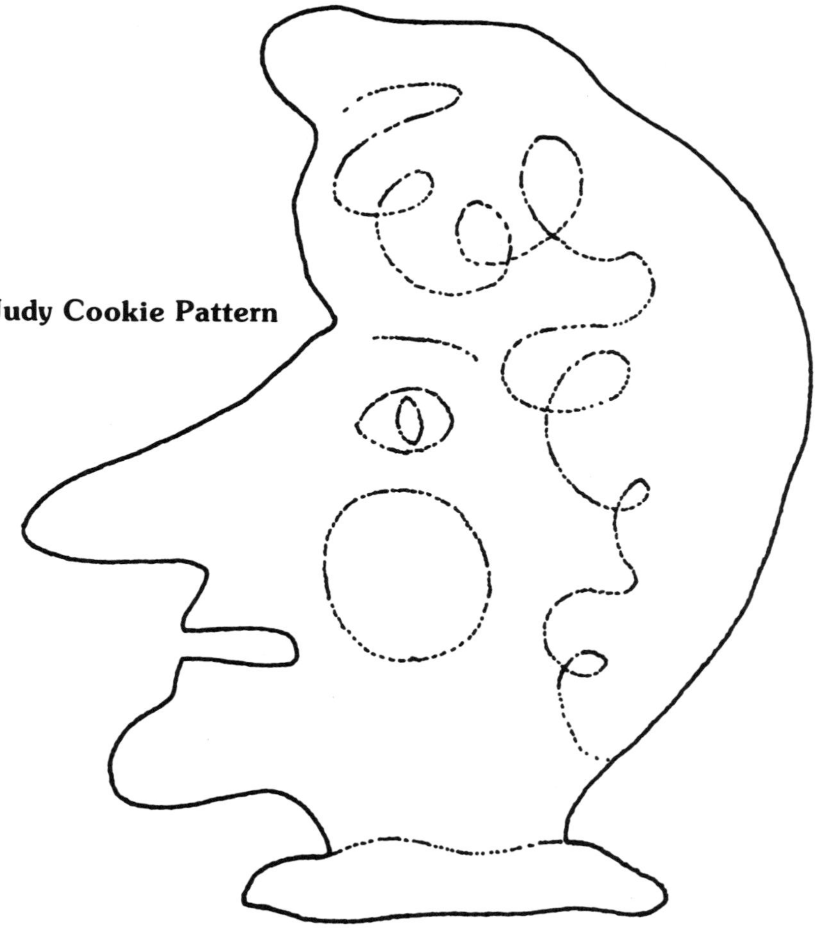

Punch Cookie

Use the Judy Cookie pattern to cut a cookie; then change the angle of the nose and the chin, pull the hair forward to make a peaked cap, and the cookie becomes Punch.

candy while still on the cookie sheet. Bake 3 to 5 minutes more. ☩ Watch closely so the candy has only enough time to melt until it is smooth. Prolonged baking will cause the colors to darken. Cool, and then strip off the wax paper. The yield varies with the size of the cookies, but it is enough for 8 children between 3 years old and kindergarten.

- Let the children taste each spice individually.
- Buy crystallized, dry, fresh root, powdered, and canned root ginger and ginger marmalade, and let the children taste, smell, and compare.
- Discuss why thicker cookies take longer to bake.
- Read the story of the Gingerbread Man.
- Compare sculpting in various media such as gingerbread, clay, Play-Doh, and Play-and-Eat Fondant (p. 91).
- Talk about stained-glass windows. Ask if the children have seen them in churches. If they haven't, visit a church or other building that has some. Request permission first.
- Make the Colored-Glass Cookies with clear "glass" (uncolored sugar candy), and compare by looking through those and the colored windows.
- Use the Colored-Glass Cookies for windows in a gingerbread house (see p. 142).
- Make a Christmas-cookie tree out of a clothes hanger. Bend into shape as shown. Tie strings or rubber bands across the "tree," and hang Colored-Glass Cookies from them. This also makes a good mobile if the cookies are coated with lacquer or hair spray to make them permanent.
- Hang the Colored-Glass Cookies on a regular Christmas tree for an old-fashioned look.

Drop Cookies

½ cup margarine
1 cup sugar
1 egg, slightly beaten
¼ cup milk
1 tsp vanilla extract
2 cups sifted flour
¼ tsp salt
2 tsp baking powder

Equipment

large bowl
mixing spoons
measuring cups
sifter
spatula
wax paper
cookie sheet
cooling rack

Yield 24 cookies

1. Preheat oven to 400°, arranging the racks to divide it in thirds so two batches of cookies can bake at once. ⊕
2. Grease cookie sheet.
3. Sift flour onto wax paper, measure, return to sifter. Add salt and baking powder. Sift together three times, to mix and aerate.
4. Cream margarine.
5. Gradually add sugar and slightly beaten egg. Blend well.
6. Add milk and vanilla. Mix.
7. Add dry ingredients gradually, and mix until well blended.
8. Drop by teaspoonfuls onto cookie sheet.
9. Bake 8 to 10 minutes, or until delicately brown and firm to the touch.
10. Remove with a spatula, and cool on a rack.

VARIATIONS

- *Whole-Wheat Cookies.* Use 1 cup sifted white flour and ¾ cup unsifted whole-wheat flour.
- *Oatmeal Cookies.* Use 1½ cups sifted white flour, and add 1⅓ cups rolled oats to the dry ingredients after they have been sifted together.
- *Orange Cookies.* Substitute orange juice for milk, and add grated rind of ½ orange.
- *Coconut Cookies.* Add 1 cup coconut, or add ½ cup to the batter and sprinkle the rest on the cookies before baking. Coconut may be tinted before baking. Enrich the experience by baking and grating the coconut in class (see p. 85).
- *Raisin Cookies.* Add 1 cup raisins to batter before baking.
- *Peanut (or Other Nut) Cookies.* Add 1 cup coarsely chopped nuts.
- *Chocolate Cookies.* Reduce flour to 1½ cups, and add ½ cup cocoa to dry ingredients.

- *Do-Your-Own-Thing Cookies.* Make a basic batter, and provide an assortment of chopped nuts, tinted coconut, butterscotch chips or chocolate chips, chocolate sprinkles, nonpareils, jelly beans, miniature marshmallows, raisins or other dried fruit (cut up), gumdrops, colored sugar, jam, or anything else that comes to mind. Drop cookies as directed, and let the children decorate their own. Bake as usual, and don't forget to make enough to send home!
- *Side-by-Side Cookies.* Two different cookie batters can be combined in a single cookie by placing ½ tsp of each kind side by side, and baking as usual.
- *Cake Cookies (Never-Fail Sour-Cream Cookies).* Use ½ package any flavor cake mix (14-ounce or 16-ounce size) and stir into ½ cup sour cream. Mix well, and drop onto greased cookie sheet. Bake 10 to 12 minutes at 375°. The recipe makes 16 cookies. There are as many variations as there are cake mixes, but brownie mix is particularly good, with or without nuts. Use ¼ cup chopped nuts if desired.

Chipmunk Chocolate Cookies
(Chocolate Chip)

2 years–kindergarten
Baking time: 10–12 minutes

½ cup margarine
½ cup sugar
¼ cup brown sugar
1 tsp vanilla extract
1 egg
1½ cups sifted flour
½ tsp salt
½ tsp baking soda
6-ounces semisweet chocolate bits

Equipment
large bowl
mixing spoon
measuring spoons
fork
sifter
spatula
wax paper
cookie sheets, greased
cooling rack

Yield 36 cookies

This is such a popular and favorite cookie that it deserves special mention.

1. Preheat oven to 350°.
2. Sift flour, measure, sift again with baking soda and salt.
3. Cream shortening.
4. Add sugar and vanilla to shortening, beating until light and fluffy.
5. Push this mixture to one side of the bowl. Break the egg into the other side of the bowl, and beat till well blended. Mix beaten egg into creamed-shortening mixture. (This saves using another bowl for beating the egg.)
6. Stir in chocolate chips and flour mixture.
7. Drop by teaspoonfuls on greased cookie sheets.
8. Bake 10 to 12 minutes.
9. Remove from cookie sheets, and cool on a rack.

VARIATIONS

- Add ½ cup chopped walnuts or ½ cup raisins.
- Use M&M's (plain or peanut) instead of chocolate chips.
- Use butterscotch chips instead of chocolate chips.
- Spread dough evenly on a greased jelly-roll pan (with sides), and bake at 350° until lightly browned. Break off in pieces when cooled.

ENRICHMENTS

- Discuss differences in the consistency of cookies, cakes, and pancakes.
- Make a Gingerbread-Cookie House with this dough (see p. 142).

- Make several varieties of cookies, and discuss the differences in taste.
- Wrap cooled cookies in aluminum foil, making sure they are airtight. Label the package with variety and date. Freeze. Explain that this is a way of storing them and keeping them fresh. After removing the cookies from the freezer, open the package and taste them frozen. Heat some in a brown paper bag at 375° for 5 minutes, or until thawed. Compare flavor, texture, and appearance of the frozen and warmed cookies. You can keep cookies in the freezer up to six months with good results, but the children might forget if you don't use them within a month.

Peanut Butter Cookies

2 years–kindergarten
Baking time: 10–12 minutes

½ cup softened margarine
½ cup peanut butter
1 cup brown or white sugar
1 egg, slightly beaten
1 tsp vanilla extract
1¼ cups sifted flour
2 tsp baking powder
½ tsp salt

Equipment
large bowl
sifter
wax paper
measuring cups
measuring spoons

1. Preheat oven to 375°. ☗
2. Sift flour, measure, and add baking powder and salt. Sift together three times, to mix well.
3. Cream margarine.
4. Add peanut butter, sugar, and slightly beaten egg to margarine. Mix thoroughly, and add vanilla.
5. Add dry ingredients gradually, and mix well.
6. Roll dough in pieces about the size of a walnut, between lightly floured hands. Place on cookie sheets about 2 inches apart.
7. Flatten by pressing twice with the under side of a lightly floured fork, to make a crisscross pattern.
8. Bake 10 to 12 minutes.
9. Remove to a rack to cool.

spatula
mixing spoon
cookie sheets, greased
cooling rack

Yield 24 cookies

VARIATIONS

- Add ½ cup chocolate chips, coconut, raisins, or chopped nuts.
- Press with the bottom of a lightly floured glass.
- Press a whole nut down in the middle of each cookie before baking.
- Use a variety of implements found in the nursery school to press different designs on the cookies, such as a potato masher, a grater, clay-working implements (well washed), thumbs (also well washed), a spoon, a cookie press. Flour them lightly before using.
- Allow the children to roll cookie dough in clean hands to make various shapes.
- Decorate cookies with raisins, nuts, and the like.
- Use other kinds of nut butters.
- Substitute whole-wheat or graham flour for the white flour.
- Substitute cocoa for ½ cup of the flour.

ENRICHMENTS

- Let children make their own peanut (or other nut) butter in the blender (see p. 68).
- Purchase a variety of nuts—raw, dry roasted, roasted, salted, unsalted, in shells, in a can, in packages.
- Purchase a variety of nuts, and compare tastes, textures, shells, and so forth.
- Study how peanuts are grown (underground), harvested, packaged, and marketed. Compare their growth with that of other nuts.
- Compare the techniques of preparing drop cookies, icebox cookies (commercial), and rolled cookies. (Drop cookies are moister than the other two. Icebox cookies have more fat than rolled, which is why they are refrigerated.)

Chocolate Grahamwiches

2 years–kindergarten
Melting time: 5 minutes

1 pound (48) graham crackers
8 ounces sour cream
12 ounces chocolate chips
1 tsp vanilla extract
⅛ tsp salt

Equipment
double boiler
wooden spoon
1 spatula or table knife for each child
hot plate
serving plate

Yield 24 Grahamwiches

1. Put chocolate chips in the top of the double boiler. Melt over 2 or 3 inches of water boiling in the bottom of the double boiler. Stir occasionally. If safe enough, permit older children to help stir.
2. Disconnect the hot plate, and remove the top of the double boiler. Take the time to discard the boiling water in the bottom. Use this as a time to explain about safety.
3. Let one of the children add the sour cream, salt, and vanilla to the melted chocolate. Let children take turns mixing the ingredients until they are well blended.
4. Using the spatulas, let the children spread ½ the graham crackers allotted to them with chocolate frosting. Then have them top each with a second cracker.
5. Let one child arrange all the Grahamwiches on a serving plate as attractively as possible.
6. Choose a second child to serve each child a napkin.
7. Choose another child to act as host or hostess to serve the Grahamwiches by passing the serving plate and allowing the other children to help themselves.

VARIATIONS

- Use butterscotch chips, milk-chocolate chips, mint chips, or a combination of these. Point out the change in flavor and color with the change of ingredients.
- Add about 4 miniature marshmallows to the icing on each of the bottom crackers before topping with the other crackers. The heat of the icing will melt the marshmallows. Point this out to the children (these are often called Somemores).
- Peanut butter thinned with a little milk to make it easier to spread also makes a good filling with or without the chocolate icing. Other possibilities include peanut butter mixed with equal parts of honey and butter, peanut butter mixed with jam or jelly, and peanut butter mixed with bananas or other fruit.

- This lesson may be used as a starting point to study the growing, harvesting, and shipping of the cacao bean, as well as the manufacture of chocolate. Illustrate your discussion with pictures.
- Have samples of the forms of chocolate and cocoa available on the market. Feel, smell, and taste them.
- Use this lesson as a starting point for a discussion of the pleasure of preparing food for others and the joy of sharing. Since this is a simple recipe, it can easily be made in large enough quantities to share with the custodians, teachers, other children, or parents at parties.
- This recipe gives a good opportunity for practice in being hosts and hostesses.

Aggression Cookies

*1 cup flour (or substitute up
to ¼ cup soy or whole-
wheat flour)*
1 cup brown sugar
1 tsp baking powder
1 cup softened margarine
2 cups oatmeal

Equipment

*extra-large bowl
measuring cups
measuring spoons
spatula
cookie sheets, greased
wax paper*

Yield 24 to 30 cookies

1. Preheat oven to 350°.
2. Dump all ingredients into the bowl.
3. Mix well with your hands, and form into 1-inch balls.
4. Place on greased cookie sheet about 2 inches apart.
5. Have each child make a fist, dip it into the flour can and "pound" his cookie to flatten it.
6. Bake 10 to 12 minutes.

In this experience, the doing is much more important than the end result. The children may even want to personalize their cookies with faces or initials before pounding.

Boom-Meringue Kisses

2 egg whites at room
 *temperature**
½ cup sugar
pinch of salt
¼ tsp cream of tartar
½ tsp vanilla extract

Equipment

large bowl with rounded
 bottom
small bowl
eggbeater
aluminum foil or brown
 paper
baking sheet
cooling rack

Yield 18 kisses

1. Preheat oven to 250°.
2. Separate whites from yolks. Put yolks in the refrigerator in the small bowl with ½ inch water covering them. (Use the yolks within two days, after pouring off the water.)
3. Add cream of tartar and salt to the egg whites.
4. Place large bowl on a folded damp cloth to keep it from slipping.
5. Beat egg whites with the eggbeater until they begin to peak.
6. Gradually add sugar by sprinkling a tablespoonful at a time over the surface of the egg whites, while continuing to beat.
7. Add vanilla.
8. Beat until very stiff peaks form (peaks must be able to stand up without flopping over).
9. Line baking sheet with brown paper or aluminum foil.
10. Spoon the meringue mixture onto the baking sheet in small rounds.
11. Bake in the center of the oven about 30 minutes, or until dry.
12. Remove from oven. Cool on rack. Remove from paper with a spatula when they are cool enough to handle.

VARIATIONS

- Cream of tartar makes the egg white and sugar combination more stable and may be omitted if you wish.
- Add a few drops of food coloring to the mixture while beating with the sugar.
- Use a variety of flavorings.

**See "Enrichments" (below) for suggestions about using the yolks.*

- Fold in ½ cup chocolate chips, shredded coconut, nuts, raisins, or drained and chopped maraschino cherries.
- Make different forms of meringues by shaping with two spoons. Make circles, squares, triangles, or animal shapes. Rounds could be made into heads, bodies, and limbs and then "glued" together with additional meringue after the first baking, and then baked again to harden the "glue."
- Fill a canvas pastry bag with the meringue mixture, and use a decorative tip for squeezing them onto the baking pan. Canvas bags can be purchased with a coupling attachment for the tips.
- Make individual meringue shells by hollowing out the centers partially with a spoon. After baking, fill with ice-cream, whipped cream, fruit, pudding, jam, jelly, or frosting.
- Meringue may be spread on soda or graham crackers, on plain cookies or raisin bread before baking.
- For gourmet cooking on the nursery-school level, make Baked Alaska. Preheat oven to 450°. Place a scoop of hard frozen ice-cream (scoop ice-cream onto a flat baking dish and return to freezer for ½ hour or more to harden before using) on a cookie or a piece of plain cake. Frost with meringue. Be sure the ice-cream is well covered by meringue. Bake about 5 minutes, or until meringue is lightly browned. Tell the children this is called Baked Alaska. One child called the helpings igloos because they can be shaped that way. Explain that the ice-cream does not melt in the short baking period because the meringue insulates it against the heat.

ENRICHMENTS

- Show the children how to separate eggs by the method given on p. 97.
- Egg whites are sufficiently beaten when they will support the weight of a whole, uncooked egg in the shell, floated on their surface. This is fun for the children to see.

- For play, whip up equal amounts of soap flakes and water until stiff. Let the children take this "meringue" outside and decorate the yard with soap-meringue flowers or other shapes. Explain that soap meringue is not for eating. Soap meringue will eventually disappear outdoors, leaving nothing damaged. It can also be tinted with food coloring or tempera.
- Beat whole eggs, and compare them to beaten whites. Call attention to the differences in volume. Explain that egg whites alone entrap more air than whole eggs can.
- Egg yolks may be used in eggnog, orange nog, or custard and can serve as the basis of another cooking lesson.
- Egg yolks can also be hard-cooked, by putting them in a custard cup and simmering them in the cup in a water bath about 10 minutes. They can then be used in salads or sandwiches. They can also be sprinkled on top of casseroles such as macaroni and cheese.

Lollipops

1 cup sugar
⅓ cup corn syrup
½ cup water
flavoring extracts
(1 tsp vanilla; or ½ tsp
coconut, lemon, or
orange; or ¼ tsp almond,
anise, or peppermint)
food coloring

Equipment

cookie sheets (covered lightly
with butter or with wax
paper)
candy thermometer
18 toothpicks or lollipop
sticks
heavy saucepan
metal tablespoon

Yield 18 lollipops

Note: This experience must be very carefully controlled, as the high temperature of the syrup can cause serious burns.

1. Cook sugar, syrup, and water in the saucepan with as little stirring as possible, to 310° on the candy thermometer (or the hard-crack stage, where syrup congeals when dropped into cold water and will crack when broken).
2. Remove cooked syrup from the heat, and add the desired coloring and flavoring with a minimum of stirring. ⊕
3. Use a metal tablespoon to quickly spoon individual spoonfuls of syrup onto cookie sheets covered with oil or wax paper. Keep them as round as possible. ⊕
4. Press toothpicks or lollipop sticks into the hot lollipops.
5. Remove lollipops from cookie sheets when cool.

VARIATIONS

- The syrup is thick enough to shape into ovals, squares, triangles, or whatever. ⊕
- Solid cookie cutters can also be used as molds. Be sure to grease them well. ⊕
- Add "treasures" to the lollipops before the candy sets—such as gumdrops, cinnamon red-hots, lemon drops or fruit-flavored hard candy.
- Make an extra supply for ornaments. Pierce a hole in each with an ice pick before the candy sets, and press a "treasure" into the candy, if you wish, for added color. When cool, thread thin cord through the holes, and hang the decorations in a window or on the Christmas tree, or else make them into a mobile.

- Discuss flavors and colors.
- Discuss the change from opaque to transparent with cooking.
- Discuss the danger of high heat and the need to be careful when cooking.
- Teach the children how to care for burns (see p. 16).

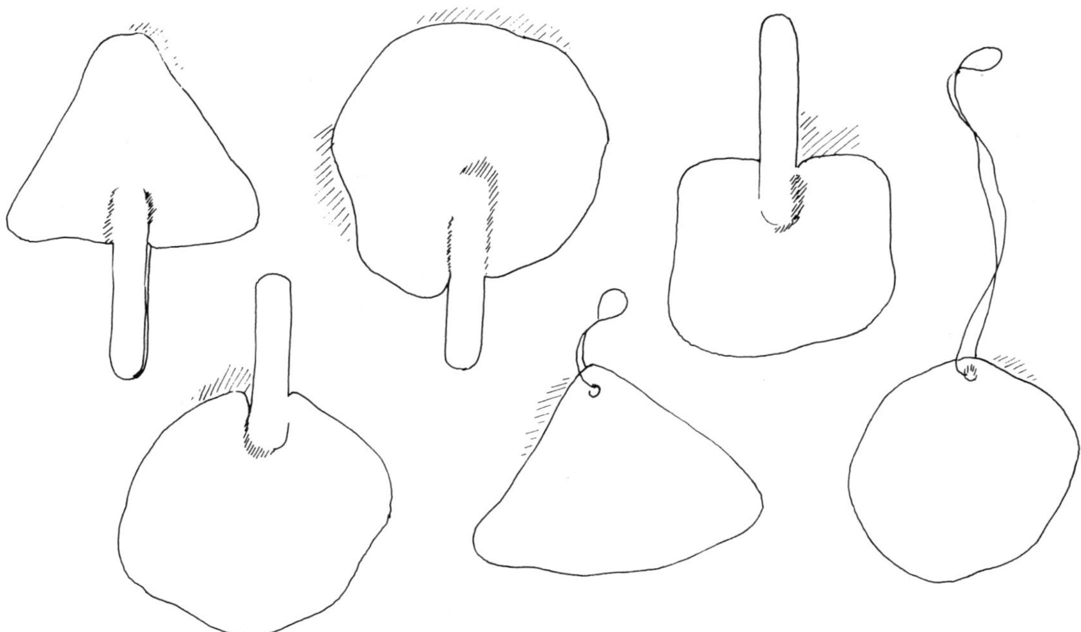

Vanilla Ice-Cream

2 cups milk
¾ cup sugar
4 tsp flour
¼ tsp salt
2 eggs
2 tsp vanilla extract
2 cups light cream
4 quarts ice cubes or
   chipped ice
ice-cream salt (rock salt)

Equipment

6-cup double boiler
small bowl
large bowl
eggbeater
ice-cream freezer (electric
   or hand-cranked; if a
   1-gallon freezer is used,
   double the recipe)
metal spoon

Yield about 1 quart ice-cream

1. Scald milk in top of double boiler. (Milk is scalded when it is just at the point of forming a skin on the surface.)
2. Mix sugar, flour, and salt in the small bowl. Slowly add the hot milk to this mixture, stirring as you pour.
3. Return mixture to the double boiler. Cook over boiling water, stirring constantly, until the mixture thickens (about 10 minutes).
4. Beat the eggs in the large bowl until well blended. Add small amounts of the hot mixture gradually, stirring constantly.
5. When all of the mixture is combined, return it to the double boiler, and continue cooking over boiling water until it is the consistency of thick cream and coats a metal spoon smoothly and evenly.
6. Remove from heat, add vanilla, and chill by putting the top of the double boiler in a bowl of cracked ice. Allow the children to stir the mixture until it is cool.
7. Add the cream, and freeze the mixture in a hand-cranked or electric freezer (see directions below).

This is a good outdoor activity, but do not allow the salt water from the freezer to come in contact with your plants or lawn, as the salt is very destructive to plants.

USING AN ICE-CREAM FREEZER

1. Before mixing the ice-cream, pour boiling water into the freezer can with the dasher in it. Allow the water to cool. Then pour off the water and allow the freezer to drain.
2. Pour the mixture to be frozen into the freezer can. Do not fill more than ¾ full, as ice-cream expands as it freezes. Adjust dasher and lid.

3. Place the can in the ice-cream freezer, and adjust the crank into position. ⊕
4. Place the freezer in a dishpan to catch any spills. You may also place a folded dish towel between freezer and pan, to hold the freezer in place more securely. ⊕
5. Fill freezer ⅓ with ice around the can before adding any ice-cream salt. Then add salt and ice in layers (1 part salt to 8 parts chipped ice, by weight, or ⅓ cup salt per quart of chipped ice, by volume). Three to four quarts crushed ice are needed for a 1-gallon freezer. Continue to add salt and ice as the ice in the freezer melts. ⊕
6. Allow children to take turns cranking until they can no longer turn the crank. An adult will probably have to finish the last stage of cranking. When an adult can no longer turn it, the ice-cream is ready.
7. Remove the ice-cream can from the freezer, and wipe it with a damp cloth.
8. Remove dasher, and scrape off the ice-cream with a spatula or spoon. (It would be a crime not to allow the children to finger taste the ice-cream from the dasher.)
9. The ice-cream can be eaten at this point, if you like it soft. Or you can ripen it by placing the ice-cream can in a refrigerator freezer at least 30 minutes. You can also ripen it in its own freezer by covering the top of the ice-cream can with wax paper, repacking it with ice and salt, and allowing it to age 30 minutes or more.

VARIATIONS

- Add 2 ounces grated sweetened chocolate to the milk in Step 1.
- Add 1 cup ripe or drained canned fruit before freezing.
- Add ½ cup chopped nuts, 1 cup chocolate chips, or ½ cup coconut before freezing.
- A few drops of food coloring may be added before freezing.
- Make ice-cream sandwiches by putting ice-cream between pairs of graham crackers or cookies. Freeze in the freezer, and use for snacks or desserts.

- Remember, for a field trip you can purchase ice-cream in many fun places, such as zoos, parks, at the beach, and from traveling trucks. Visit an ice-cream store or factory. Be sure to have samples for tasting.
- Make sundaes, sodas, shakes, or malts using various flavors of ice-cream and toppings.
- Have a "make your own sundae" party. Let children select their own ice-cream flavors and toppings.
- Let ice-cream melt, and discuss the changes in texture, temperature, and flavor.
- Set up an ice-cream stand, using a table or a large packing case made into a "store." Let some children fill the ice-cream cones with a scoop, and let the rest of the children purchase the ice-cream from them with play money or "money" made of strips of paper with numbers written on them. If a toy truck is available, one child can use it to be an ice-cream vendor.
- Use this as a starting point for a study of milk and milk products (see "Enrichment," p. 72).

SOURCES OF ENRICHMENT MATERIALS

These organizations offer a variety of charts, pamphlets, posters, photographs, filmstrips, and recipes. Since conditions and costs are ever-changing, it might be wise to write, asking what materials are currently available, before making a specific request. Inquire about new materials, and ask to be put on their mailing lists. When they mail to a school, many such organizations will send the material with the bill included, if there is a charge.

American Dental Association
  222 East Superior St.
  Chicago, Ill. 60611
  posters, pamphlets

American Institute of Baking
  400 East Ontario St.
  Chicago, Ill. 60611
  posters, pamphlets, recipes

American Meat Institute
  59 East Van Buren
  Chicago, Ill. 60605
  posters, pamphlets, recipes

American Sheep Producer's Council
  200 Clayton St.
  Denver, Colo. 80206
  posters, pamphlets, recipes

California Beef Council
  363 Brewster Ave.
  Redwood City, Ca. 94063
  posters, pamphlets, recipes

California Dairy Council
  3900 West Third St.
  Los Angeles, Ca. 90020
  nutritional aids, posters, pamphlets

California Fisheries Institute
  300 South Ferry St., Rm. 2016
  Terminal Island, Ca. 90731
  posters, pamphlets, recipes

Campbell Soup Company
  Box 391, Campbell Place
  Camden, N.J. 08101
  posters, pamphlets, recipes

Cereal Institute
  135 South LaSalle St.
  Chicago, Ill. 60603
  posters, pamphlets, recipes

Del Monte Kitchens
  Box 3575
  San Francisco, Ca. 94119
  posters, pamphlets, recipes

Diamond Walnut Kitchens
  47 Kearny St.
  San Francisco, Ca. 94108
  posters, pamphlets, recipes

Edcom Systems, Inc.
  745 Alexander Rd.
  Princeton, N.J. 08540
  catalog of small-scale kitchen items

General Foods Kitchens
250 North St.
White Plains, N.J. 10602
posters, pamphlets, recipes

General Mills
Box 300
Minneapolis, Minn. 54480
posters, pamphlets, recipes

Glidden-Durkee
900 Union Commerce Building,
Cleveland, Ohio 44115
posters, pamphlets, recipes

Heinz-USA
Box 57
Pittsburgh, Pa. 15230
posters, pamphlets, recipes

Hershey Foods
Hershey, Pa. 17033
posters, pamphlets, recipes

Hunt-Wesson Foods
Box 1008
Fullerton, Ca. 92632
posters, pamphlets, recipes

Idaho Potato Commission
Box 1068
Boise, Idaho 83701
posters, pamphlets, recipes

Kansas Wheat Commission
1021 North Main St.
Hutchinson, Kans. 67501
posters, pamphlets, recipes

National Dairy Council
111 North Canal St.
Chicago, Ill. 60606
posters, pamphlets

National Livestock and Meat Board
3650 Wabash Ave.
Chicago, Ill. 60603
posters, pamphlets, recipes

Nutrition USA
Pueblo, Colo. 81009
*Food Is More Than Just Something
to Eat* (pamphlet)

Oscar Meyer Meat Company
Madison, Wis. 53701
posters, pamphlets, recipes

Parents' Magazine Films, Inc.
52 Vanderbilt Ave.
New York, N.Y. 10017
filmstrips on nutrition

The Polished Apple
3742 Seahorn Dr.
Malibu, Ca. 90265
filmstrips and cassettes

Poultry and Egg Association,
National Board
18 South Michigan Ave.
Chicago, Ill. 60603
posters, pamphlets, recipes

Quaker Oats
Consumer Services Department
Merchandise Mart Plaza
Chicago, Ill. 60654
posters, pamphlets, recipes

Rice Council
Box 22802
Houston, Tex. 77027
posters, pamphlets, recipes

Society for Nutrition Education
2140 Shattuck Ave., Suite 110
Berkeley, Ca. 94704
*lists of sources of teaching aids about
nutrition*

Sunkist Growers
Box 2706 Terminal Annex
Los Angeles, Ca. 90030
posters, pamphlets, recipes

U.S. Department of Agriculture,
Food and Nutrition Service
14th St. and Independence Ave.
Washington, D.C. 20250
Good Foods Coloring Book (CMS 61),
and other materials

U.S. Government Printing Office
Washington, D.C. 20402
Katy's Coloring Book (about drugs and health, 35¢)

U.S. Department of Health, Education and Welfare
Washington, D.C. 20201
pamphlets

University of Kentucky
Cooperative Extension Service
College of Agriculture
South Limestone St.
Lexington, Ky. 40506
Johnny Goes to Nutritionland (coloring book for preschoolers)

Vitamin Information Bureau
383 Madison Ave.
New York, N.Y. 10017
filmstrips and cassettes, wall charts, pamphlets

Western Growers Association
3091 Wilshire Blvd.
Los Angeles, Ca. 90010
posters, pamphlets, recipes

FURTHER READING ON NUTRITION

Bogert, L. Jean; Briggs, G.; and Calloway, D. *Nutrition and Physical Fitness*. Philadelphia: W. B. Saunders Co., 1973.

Guthrie, Helen A. *Introductory Nutrition*. Saint Louis: C. V. Mosby Co., 1975.

Howe, Phyllis S. *Basic Nutrition in Health and Disease*. Philadelphia: W. B. Saunders Co., 1971.

Lowenberg, Mirriam E., et al. *Food and Man*. New York: John Wiley and Sons, Inc., 1974.

McWilliams, Margaret. *Nutrition for the Growing Years*. New York: John Wiley and Sons, Inc., 1967.

Robinson, Corrine. *Fundamentals of Normal Nutrition*. New York: Macmillan Publishing Co., Inc., 1973.

Thomas, Susan B. *Nutrition and Learning in Preschool Children*. Urbana, Ill.: ERIC Clearinghouse on Early Childhood Education, 1972.

U.S. Congress, Senate, Select Committee on Nutrition and Human Needs. *Hearings*, 91st Cong., 2d sess., 1970. Washington, D.C.: U.S. Government Printing Office.

Wilson, Eva D., et al. *Principles of Nutrition*. New York: John Wiley and Sons, Inc., 1975.

Winick, Myron, ed. *Nutrition and Development*. New York: John Wiley and Sons, Inc., 1972.

INDEX